PRACTICAL CHRISTIANITY:

Devotional Reflections on the Book of James

Wayne Brouwer

In memory of Grandpa (Arend Ubbo) Brouwer who often reminded me,

"We get too soon old and too late smart."

PREFACE

One of my earliest experiences of group Bible study involved eight of us during our high school years on a summer's mission project using a little booklet to help us think about Christian living as expressed in the letter of James. Two things impressed me then, and they impress me yet today. First, James writes about Christian faith as if it ought to make sense and ought to make a difference. Second, his teachings are really a kind of stream-of-consciousness presentation of rambling exhortations that hit a bunch of tender spots, but don't develop a comprehensive package of Christian lifestyle.

Both of these impressions sit well with me. I am more and more convinced that we tend to institutionalize and theologize Christian faith in the church, and that we need often simply to get back to living it. And living out our relationship with God is a kind of rambling, stream-of-consciousness, day-by-day exercize in developing Christian character. There is no complete package that we can either buy or beg. James helps me think again that life is both simple and complex at the same time, and that the best way Home is with a Friend.

I hope these devotional reflections will help you wrestle with the same issues and impressions. In fact, I hope to meet you some day, and see a little of James' wisdom coloring your complexion as it has mine.

All the best…

Wayne Brouwer

INTERPRETIVE BACKGROUND

For some biblical figures we have quite a bit of historical information—David, Paul, Peter. For some biblical books we have a great deal of textual information to help us understand their form and style—the covenant literature of Exodus and Deuteronomy, for example, or Hebrew poetry, or the four-fold gospel record.

With James, however, we find little of either. There are but a few snippits and hints about James, the brother of Jesus, from early church records; certainly not enough to build a complex portrait of the man. Furthermore, there are no notes in the text of the letter to pin it in either time or space, nor sufficient data from the churches gradual collection of New Testament documents to help us clearly define it origins.

Yet there are enough bits and pieces and textual allusions to bring most scholars to some similar conclusions about this short letter of exhortation and encouragement. First, while there were a number of men in the Jerusalem church community of the first century who had the position or ability to write a letter like this, it seems reasonable to listen to the testimony of those who identify him as the James of Acts 15. This James is not the brother of John, the two of whom were known as "Sons of Zebedee" in the gospels, and called together to be part of the Twelve disciples of Jesus. That James had been murdered by Herod already in Acts 12. The James of Acts 15 was a biological half-brother to Jesus; he had grown up in the same home as Jesus, and experienced a lifetime of interaction with the Messiah. This James became primary leader of the church in Jerusalem, and spoke with authority among its broader leadership at the gathering described in Acts 15.

Second, it is difficult to date the letter or to clearly mark its occasion. There are, however, a few hints that seem to help us make some calculated suggestions. For one thing, the letter carries many similarities to speeches and conversations of Jesus recorded in the gospels (especially the Sermon on the Mount of Matthew 5-7), leading us to believe that it was written not that long after Jesus had returned to heaven, and by a person who had spent a great deal of time with Jesus. Furthermore, the direct reference to this letter's being sent "to the twelve tribes scattered among the nations" (1:1) and the connections with Jewish wisdom expressions (e.g., Proverbs, Ecclesiastes) seem to confirm that this letter was intended to be read in its first editions by Jewish Christians. Along with that, the several references to the social tensions between rich and poor, and the fact that no reference is made to Jerusalem's destruction, point to a date early in the church when economic and social issues were a major concern, and much of the identity of the Jewish Christian community extended from its Jerusalem base. Finally the clear designation of this letter as a type of widely distributed exhortation fits with the story of Acts 15, since the leaders of the church wanted, on that occasion, to send out a statement of common understandings and preferred behaviors for Christian living.

For these reasons many biblical scholars have suggested that we read this letter as written by James, the brother of Jesus, who gave primary leadership to the Christian community in Jerusalem during its formative years; and that we see the letter itself as quite possibly a longer, more personal and pastoral letter sent along with the specific edicts circulated by the church leaders in Acts 15. These are sensible thoughts to have mind as we read the letter of James together.

1

Labels

"James, a servant of God and of the Lord Jesus Christ, to the twelve tribes scattered among the

nations..." (James 1:1)

Robert Wuthnow remembers his first day of teaching at Princeton University. He walked into a seminar room without a class list and passed a sheet of paper around the room, asking students to write their names. When the page was returned Wuthnow found he had received more than he had requested. Next to each person's name was an apostrophe and a two-digit number: *John Alexander '76; Frederick Thompson '77; Charles Francis Lovell '76; Philip Norton III '76...*

It didn't take Professor Wuthnow long to figure it out: the numbers corresponded with the year that each student expected to graduate from Princeton. "Interesting," he thought. "Once a person enrolls at Princeton he or she gains a new identity. There is a vast network of Princeton people all over the world, and they know each other by their labels—a name and a date."

"Alma Mater"

For more than two centuries it has been like that: once you are a part of the brotherhood of Princeton, you belong. You have an identity. In fact, at the start of each school year, Princeton people gather from the far reaches of travel for the annual "P-rade." Banners are lifted for each year of the past, the present and the future, and Princeton people march proudly in their regiments, forming links in a chain forged year by year at this, their *alma mater.*

The term *alma mater* originated in the ancient Greek legends of Ceres and Cybele. These women, according to the story tellers, gathered homeless and sick children and mothered them back to life, loved them back to health, and gave them a place in society with a name and an identity. "Alma maters," the Greeks called these two, Ceres and Cybele: "Fostering mothers."

It is with that in mind that Princeton people march each year under the banner of their *alma mater*. Princeton has mothered them into a common life.

Crying for Mother

Wuthnow reflected on this fascinating expression of our human need. It reminds us, he said, how important it is for each of us to gain an identity. We need to know whom we are, not just within ourselves, but also in the context of a social system that matters. In fact, when Wuthnow conducted extensive surveys, he found that roughly 90% of all people give their highest priority and most energy in life to the task of "finding themselves" and then projecting a unique personal identity.

Our obsession with personal identity is betrayed by the manner in which we introduce ourselves. We want people to know our names. We tell them what work we do, or what successes we have accomplished. We trace our family roots and community backgrounds. All of this becomes a statement of who we are.

Wuthnow also said that, unfortunately, most of us never do become fully aware of who we are. Inside we carry about with us great insecurities. We secretly believe that we project more than we can deliver, and that much of our public persona is deceitful.

For that reason we keep searching for *alma maters*, "fostering mothers" who will take us in, and dress our egos, and give us names of significance. We run, said Wuthnow, from this possession to that career, from this title to that university degree, from this accomplishment to that social club, hoping that somewhere among them we can find the mother who will tell us who we truly are.

Badges of Honor

That is why labels are important to us. Generic brands may be fine for toilet paper and canned soup, but humans need a product stamp that restores their sense of holy self.

James seemed to be aware of that when he penned this letter. Four labels he gives, two for self, two for his readers, all for the church. *A servant of God*—at home in the household of the Master of the Universe. *A servant of the Lord Jesus Christ*—loved into living. *To the twelve tribes*—a heritage of divine grace and encircling community. *Scattered among the nations*—pilgrims with a mission.

Those are mighty fine banners under which to march!

2

99.4% Pure Joy

"Consider it pure joy, my brothers, whenever you face trials of many kinds..." (James 1:2)

Those in marketing say that there are a number of rules to follow when trying to sell a product. One is to keep it simple—the more technical data and variety of informative details you give to the prospective buyer, the less likely that you will hold her attention or convince him of his need for your product. Another rule is to accentuate the positive. Cutting down the competition sways few people, except in election campaigns. A third rule is to pinpoint one unique distinction about your product that sets it apart from all imitators.

Try This!

Proctor & Gamble Company hit the jackpot in advertising, many years ago, when they followed those three rules precisely in marketing their Ivory soap. People remember the commercials yet today: a form shaped like the Ivory soap bar, and a hand pouring into it what was touted to be *pure* liquid soap. The pouring didn't stop until the mold was filled. Then the announcer, in a quiet but authoritative voice, declared that researchers had analyzed Ivory soap and found it to be 99.44% pure. What more could anyone want?

Pure soap is a common luxury. Pure joy is   an uncommon dream. Much that passes in the name of religion has a feel-bad quality about it, producing either warped psyches or overgrown spiritual brats. Christian psychologist Wayne Oates made that point in his book *When Religion Gets Sick*. In it he told horror stories of those who take grace and turn it into law, and of those who use God or the church or the Bible as moral clubs with which to browbeat others into certain patterns of behavior.

If religion gets sick, all its promises of inner joy and peace vanish. God becomes an ogre who taunts us into failure and leers at our lapses with the relish of an executioner.

Mixed Message

Homiletics professor Gerald Kennedy had a sharp word for those who diluted or destroyed the pure joy of the gospel with vitriolic attacks of unrighteous indignation. He told of a preacher who devoted his career to being against everything. Each week his sermon condemned this idea and challenged that notion. He was always ranting against this and clearly not in favor of that; he was down on these people and alienated from those.

For a while, said Kennedy, his church grew and grew. People like to listen to someone who gets them riled up, who stirs their blood and who calls them out to war. They enjoy the feeling that they are on the right side, and even more they have an urge to believe that everyone else is wrong. The preacher Kennedy wrote about made his congregation feel so good about feeling so bad.

But after he retired the crowds disappeared, and the church withered and died. When no one was there any longer to tell them what they were against, they didn't know what they were for. They had no reason to carry on. It was easy to feed on criticism and guilt and self-righteousness when their harsh preacher was dancing in the pulpit, throwing stones in every direction. But when the stones stopped flying, the people didn't know what they stood for. Hatred burned them out and they had never learned to love.

Ad Campaign

In a sense, the message of James stands as an ad for the pure joy of Christianity over against a variety of lesser brands that mix the substance of true religion with smut and dross. Fred Allen, in his radio comedies of a bygone era, often encouraged his listeners, "You only live once, but if you do it right, once is enough." That is true not only of life generally, but especially of the spiritual winds that lift the sails of our souls.

Still, virtues are rarely experienced or expressed in pure form by pursuing them directly. No one becomes humble merely by trying to act in humble ways. Nor does anyone produce courage solely through pumping up one's ego. Patience probably comes least to the one who thinks about it, and graciousness rarely to him who attempts to act graciously. Unless the heart breathes with these virtues, our feeble attempts at chivalry ring hollow.

So too with joy, especially of the "pure" kind. It happens, as James suggests, when one reflects on evil circumstances of life and realizes that these need not dictate who I am or how I will respond. To put it in basic terms, when the mold is properly shaped, God will take care of pouring into it the refined substance of joy, at least 99.44% pure.

Browning said it this way, in one of his poems: "God's in His heaven—All's right with the world." That is neither a scientific analysis nor a weighted political poll. It is a judgment of faith.

3

Perseverance

"...you know that the testing of your faith develops perseverance." (James 1:3)

We all love stories of courage:

- Francis Parkman suffered from both arthritic muscles and poor eyesight. He could work only five minutes at a time, scrawling huge letters on his manuscript, yet he managed to complete a massive twenty-volume historical masterpiece.

- Thomas Edison labored virtually non-stop in his attempts to find a way to develop two-way transmissions on a single telephone line. Suffering from exhaustion, he was ready to give up. Yet persistence won out and on the twenty-second day he found a solution that gave birth to modern telephony.

- Michael Blake left home at 17 to make his mark in the literary and cinematic world. He wrote more than twenty screenplays and numerous other stories and novels, but received only rejection slips for twenty-five years. Then, finally, the whole world shouted his praise when his *Dances with Wolves* told a tale everyone needed to hear.

It is always wonderful when perseverance wins out over huge odds: Former Secretary of State Henry Kissinger made more than twenty secret trips to China before he was at last able to open new diplomatic ties between East and West; Colonial Sanders met rejection one hundred twelve times as he pitched his fried chicken recipe until finally selling his first franchise; Joe Wilson spent ten years attempting to make ink stick to paper and then one day stumbled on the secret that turned "Xerox" into a household name.

Winners and Losers

Those stories are inspiring, aren't they?

Maybe so in retrospect, although I have to confess it is hard for me to get motivated by the end results of successful ventures when there is no guarantee that the outcome will be the same for me. In my career as pastor I have seen too much of failure even among those most full of faith and confidence to jump blithely into "Pollyanna" mode. I watched a young couple bury three newborn sons in three successive years on foreign soil, far from family, in spite of the best efforts of medical science. I've heard the desperate cries of women who cannot get over the horrible pain of what fathers did to them in the secrecy of childhood bedrooms. I've seen robust faith degenerate through years of setbacks and loss.

Elaine Pagels, in retelling the story of a particular sect of early Christians, says, "History is told by the winners." There is a lot of truth in that. Who remembers the losers? Who keeps tabs on the has-beens? Who records the disasters of those who fade away under pressure or disaster?

History is told by the winners, and losers, even those who began with confidence and enthusiasm, are swallowed by the margins and forgotten. Even their tears are forgotten.

Perseverance Pays Off

Still, the stories of those who succeed dangle before us like candy. Norman Vincent Peale once described a scene where a young woman stared in disbelief as the Queen of England, Elizabeth II, approached her in open sight of thousands of people and hundreds of television cameras, and crowned her tennis champion of the world. It was the culmination of a powerful story of perseverance, since young Althea Gibson was born in poverty and suffered crushing childhood illnesses that left her muscles weak and her limbs twisted.

It was the perseverance of Althea's mother that made the difference. Mrs. Gibson one day pointed to a rock across the yard and asked her daughter, "Do you see that stone down there by the barn?" The girl did. It was huge, Althea remembered, and looked like an overgrown potato. "I want you to go down there and bring it up to the house," said her mother, "so we can use it as a step by the kitchen door."

The girl sobbed and protested. "Mommy!" she lamented, "I'm so weak that I can hardly even walk down there! How can I possibly move a stone that big?"

Her mother persisted, and simply said, "You can do it! I have confidence in you! You'll figure something out."

Indeed, inch by inch, rolling and tugging and pushing, the young lass moved that rock to the house. It took her two months to do what a healthy child would have accomplished in fifteen minutes. But as she tussled with the stone Althea's muscles strengthened and her limbs straightened. Surprised by her new energy, she began a rigorous training program that led to tennis and ultimately to Wimbledon. It was there that Althea Gibson was crowned victor by the Queen of England before an awestruck world.

Another Dimension

When I first read Althea's story I had the same initial diffidence that other "success" stories often bring. But there was something in Althea's response both to her struggles and to their outcome that wrinkled with less tinsel. In Althea's view the story revolved not around her own ability to see things through, but rather focused on her mother's "constant faithfulness and abiding love," to use a term pirated from a marriage ceremony. Perseverance was, for her, not so much the confidence of winning at Wimbledon or inventing something new or succeeding in business. Rather, it was being able to count on a relationship that would never let her down, even if she did not accomplish great things. The success was in being worthy of significance because she was loved, and not becoming worthy of love because she achieved some kind of "success."

That is probably what James has in mind as well when he writes about developing perseverance in faith. Perhaps we will be fortunate enough to celebrate our dreams come true. Yet whether we win or lose in life, faith's perseverance reminds us that God will always be there for us. That's reward enough for both time and eternity.

4

Growing Up

"Perseverance must finish its work so that you may be mature and complete, not lacking anything."

(James 1:4)

As a young father, I was rather excited by the future. If our daughters would have been true to their dreams, we would have a waitress, a lawyer, a nurse, a teacher, a ballet dancer, a professional singer, a police officer, a doctor, a celebrated author, a painter, a fireman, a minister, a flight-crew attendant, a pilot, an astronaut, an actress, a homemaker, and a professional soccer player in our family. Moreover, such things would not have happened because our three girls would marry boys, and thus expand the number of people available for all these careers. After all, at the time they knew that they did not like boys. All these occupations emerged as hopes and wishes and goals of our three. I couldn't wait to have daughters who will care for us, teach us, entertain us, support us, help us travel, serve us and clean up after us! It would be sort of like having Nancy Drew, Tom Swift, the Hardy Boys, Harry Potter, Supergirl and Buckaroo Bonsai wrapped up together in three wonderful persons!

We have all played the game "What do you want to be when you grow up?" It is fun when we are children, but it begins to lose its delight as we grow older and still are not sure that we have chosen well or wisely. Our daughters used to envy grown ups because we could do, in their words, "anything you

17

want!" How little they knew of the restrictions that hemmed us in with greater grip than any childhood prison.

Lost Childhood

Roy Drusky sang of that lost innocence years ago in a reflection he called *Long, Long Texas Road*: "I've been up and I've been down," he crooned. "I've worked the fields, I've plowed the ground. I've borne the strain and pressure till I thought I might explode. Now I search for childhood days of model ships and rocket planes, when the days stretched out before me like a long, long Texas road."

His refrain was a whimsical reminiscence:

Oh, that long, long Texas road's about a million miles or so…

When you're just a child there ain't no time but now.

Must have lost that long old road seven hundred years ago,

And I'd find it once again if I knew how.

I've often felt, with Drusky, that I've missed something along the way and I would like to retrace my steps now and again in order truly to find myself. Yet, with him, I know that God gives us only one chance to walk through time. We may delight in trying to find something of Peter Pan in our hearts, and steal away in daydream moments to Neverland in our playful thoughts. But time marches forward, not back, and age requires of us something that we may not grab hold on willfully.

Still, there is a difference between growing older and growing up. Growing older changes our bodies, while sometimes leaving our personalities underdeveloped and childish. Years ago Dutch pastor Cornelis Gilhuis penned a little book of meditations called *Conversations on Growing Older* (Eerdmans, 1977) to encourage maturity along with advancing age. He spoke sharply to those who become crotchety and cantankerous in their senior years, and gently encouraged the deeper adult expressions of peace and patience and piety. Maturity, he said, does not always pair itself with age.

Reaching for God

Mark Twain wrote that when he was fourteen he thought his father was an idiot. "But when I turned twenty-one," he added, "I was amazed at how much the old man had learned in seven years!" Obviously Twain himself had learned a thing or two by that time. One hopes we all will learn such things as time goes by.

The strangest thing about maturity is that it sneaks up on us best when we don't pursue it overmuch. We can do little about age, but maturity comes quickest to those who do not wrestle it down. Malcolm Muggeridge said it beautifully in his own reflections on growing old. He told of nights when he found himself in bed, yet somehow suspended between this world and the next, sensing that things glow with the lights of Augustine's *City of God*. His thoughts in that moment of quiet harmony were not about himself, he said, but rather about how wonderful it was to be alive and to know that all things come together and find their purpose in the hand of God.

I have an idea that James would smile in agreement.

5

Wisdom

"If any of you lacks wisdom, he should ask God, who gives generously to all without finding fault, and it will be given to him." (James 1:5)

In H. G. Wells' tale "The Queer Story of Brownlow's Newspaper," it is November 10, 1931, when Mr. Brownlow returns to his apartment at the end of work and sits down to read his evening paper. As he takes the wrapped bundle in his hands he thinks it feels different than usual. Looking at the address he notices that it was supposed to go to an Evan O'Hara. Still, if he got Mr. O'Hara's newspaper it is likely that this is only a minor mix-up, and that Mr. O'Hara is already enjoying Mr. Brownlow's paper over a cup of tea. So Mr. Brownlee unwraps the daily journal and settles in.

Soon, however, he is caught by the strangeness of this paper. The paper is smoother than usual to the touch and the photographs are in color. More significantly, the news itself doesn't seem to make sense, tossing off names of countries he's never heard of, world leaders he can't remember rising to power, and contraptions he's never seen. As he turns again to the front page Mr. Brownlow notes the date: November 10, 1971. Forty years into the future!

Instant Insight

He scours the pages with growing interest and amusement. The world is governed by something called a Federal Board. Fashions have changed. Environmental concerns and conservation seem to be top priorities. Mr. Brownlow laughs to himself, sure that this is some elaborate hoax cleverly fobbed off on him. Still, in the middle of the night his nuisance paper troubles him, and he tears out a section to show to his friend in the morning.

When he wakes, however, the cleaning woman has arrived. She threw the paper out with the garbage and now only his scrap remains.

Wells ends his story there, leaving the reader nursing an uneasy speculation. What could have caused the time warp? Is there a Wisdom that transcends time and injects enough prophetic caution into the system to keep us from self-destructing? Does Someone in the universe know what is going on? Are we dabbling at things like rats caught in a mysterious maze while all around us, beyond the light of the stars, a host of giant Presences compare notes and chuckle at our limitations and stupidity? Do they tantalize us in moments like Mr. Brownlow's serendipitous encounter by dangling carrots of prophetic insight before us?

Infrequent Intelligence

Obviously wisdom is in shorter supply than we might hope. Politicians blow clouds of cryptic absolutes, pleasing all and none. Marriages begin with confident vows, only to end with hollow suggestions that "we made a mistake." My Grandpa used to shake his head and say, "We get too soon old and too late smart." Hegel summarized well the plight of the human race: "What experience and history teach us is this—that people and governments never have learned anything from history."

Where is wisdom to be found? Will someone drop a "Shining Path" from the heavens to provide insight rather than bloodshed?

James' letter is something of a New Testament version of Proverbs. What he says about wisdom fits well with that earlier biblical collection. Most of the Proverbs are maxims and sayings that summarize clear-headed approaches to living. Yet the introduction to the book of Proverbs is essentially a contest. In chapters 1-9 two women ("Wisdom" and "Folly" are both feminine nouns in the Hebrew language) attempt to woo the author's coming-of-age son. What makes Wisdom a winner is not so much that she can bring wealth or power or fame; rather, Wisdom's great asset is her link to divine love.

Winsome Wisdom

Intelligence can be brittle and harsh. Like Mr. Brownlow's magical newspaper it can tell us information without helping us truly live. Experience, likewise, may be a teacher that turns us more mean and spiteful than gracious and caring.

Only true wisdom is rooted in divine goodness and mercy. It is not as concerned with data as it is with persons who can use or abuse that data. It is not as worried about information as it is about how that information warms human hearts. It is not as focused on facts and figures as it is on relationships and healing.

Tests and examinations for knowledge of the intellect can sometimes encourage people to "find fault," as James puts it. But a relationship of significance with God goes beyond "finding fault" to encouragement. That's probably why James, at the start of his letter, echoes the opening testimony of the Proverbs, "The fear of the Lord is the beginning of wisdom." (Proverbs 1:7)

6

In Two Minds

"When he asks, he must believe and not doubt, because he who doubts is like a wave of the sea, blown and tossed by the wind. That man should not think he will receive anything from the Lord; he is a double-minded man, unstable in all he does." (James 1:6-8)

One Chinese word-symbol for "doubt" is a caricature of a person with each foot in a different canoe. If the waters are calm and the canoes are tied securely, it is possible for the person to stand like that indefinitely. But if those canoes are adrift on the swelling tides of the sea or scrambling down the whitewaters of a raging torrent, someone positioned so precariously would topple quickly.

Cecil Beaton pictures it well in his short story "The Settee." Violet and Dorothy prowl and antique shop and find a marvelous old French style long wooden bench called a settee. Dorothy thinks it is "Louise-Seize," and therefore extremely valuable. When she finds that she can get it for a very inexpensive price, she convinces Violet to allow her to buy it as a gift for Violet.

Second Thoughts

Of course, the value of the piece weighs heavily in Dorothy's mind, and soon she begins to dream of ways to get it back for herself. After all, she was the one who found it in the first place. Sharing her obsession with family friend Colonel Coddington, they scheme together to trick Violet into surrendering custody of the piece by declaring it a worthless imitation.

The tables are turned, however, when Colonel Coddington inspects the supposed antique and declares that it is, in fact, only a cheap copy of the famous Louis-Sieze style, and certainly not valuable at all. Dorothy's greed and obsession deflate rapidly.

The next day she laughingly relates the whole tale to George. Then the roller coaster ride begins all over again as George informs Dorothy that the Colonel's ability to appraise anything is sheer quackery, and he wouldn't know art from imitation. George, who has seen the settee, knows that it is indeed a rare and valuable piece. After all, he himself owns an antique shop where a bench twin to Violet's sits in the window with a huge price tag. Dorothy's obsessive greed is fired anew, and passionate covetousness surges through her veins.

Inner Turmoil

There Beaton ends the story, allowing Dorothy's mood-swings to rip apart her heart. She is the epitome of a "double-minded" person of the kind James describes: thinking this, yet believing that at the same time.

Obviously, in Beaton's tale, a remedy might readily be found. Dorothy needed only to contract the services of a bona fide antique appraiser in order to sort fact from fantasy. Once she knew the actual sticker price, the doubt of two-mindedness would be resolved and she could devise further plots and strategies to deal with Violet in a Beaton-eqse sequel.

The deeper doubt that James talks of, though, is not so easily settled. Although it operates in a fashion similar to Dorothy's devious dualism, there is no human expert available to sift Truth from Lie and firmly pin faith securely to the mast of heaven's sail.

The seas always roll, in life's journey, and the pounding waves beg their share of the soul's cargo. And those of us who have experienced significant doubts in the uncharted waters of our voyage find these verses in James' letter very harsh and most intimidating.

Certainly it is true that many Christians are single-minded and clearly aware of the brilliant sunshine of God's love, rarely deviating from paths of focused faith and purposeful existence. Yet while some folks have a "summery" sort of spirituality, according to Martin Marty in his devotional reflections on the Psalms, many of us know only or often *A Cry of Absence* (Harper & Row, 1983). For those who wrestle often the blasts of chilling doubt and wrestle for direction under gray and forbidding skies, the Absence of God seems more apparent than his Presence. John Crowe Ransom put it this way:

Two evils, monstrous either one apart,

Possessed me, and were long and loath at going;

A cry of Absence, Absence, in the heart,

And in the wood the furious winter blowing.

Taming the Gales

When the Absence of God shouts louder than his Presence, few who feel faith can escape the winds of doubt. Fortunately these verses are not all that James has to say on the subject. There will come moments of brilliance and insight further along in his letter of encouragement. Perhaps, even, the harshness of his judgment here will challenge those of us with wintry spirits to take a second look at our perennial insecurities of faith.

Still, the best that comes from James' descriptive wisdom about faith and doubt here is the intensity of his diagnosis regarding the emotional toll wreaked on hearts that waffle indecisively between trust and despair. Life is hard for those of us who linger often between two minds.

Without the larger context of grace binding the fraying edges of our souls, more ships of self would visit Davey Jones' locker than would reach the Haven of Rest. Fortunately the One who stilled the storms on the Sea of Galilee is able yet to tame the troubling tides for those who cry out in winter's night. I know it experientially.

25

7

Juxtaposition

"The brother in humble circumstances ought to take pride in his high position. But the one who is rich should take pride in his low position…" (James 1:9-10)

Roland Pertwee's short story "The Voice That Said 'Good Night'" tells of Philip Gaylor's murder. One morning he was found dead in his chair, neck twisted and broke. Who could have done it?

It might have been anyone, said Charles Crichton to the investigating officer. After all, Philip Gaylor "was the kind of beast who kept his soul in his trousers pocket, along with his other small change."

That is an amazing description of a man! According to Crichton, Philip Gaylor was spiritually bankrupt, and his soul was reduced to a plaything he could pocket with his other cheap coins. As Mr. Gaylor's wealth increased, his heart nearly evaporated and his life became a shade shuffling expensive shadows.

Pulling the Plug

Money is a power in our lives. We have all felt it feed our greed or suck like a leech at our souls. In our consumer-oriented society it has to be disarmed or it will consume us with credit card debt and gambling addictions. One family in our neighborhood is painfully climbing out of an over-buying hole.

Another friend now spends more time at Gamblers' Anonymous meetings than he does in church.

Jaques Ellul, the deeply religious French social critic, offered some hopeful suggestions in his book *Money and Power* (IVP, 1984). Ellul said that there are three ways we can learn to defuse the power of money in our lives.

First, in all the issues of life, said Ellul, we must choose to side with the human dimension rather than the economic. In other words, we have to refocus the glasses of our heart's eyes to see persons before profits. Economic problems have to become, for us, human relations successes. People always matter more than the bottom line on bills.

Quenching the Fires

Second, said Ellul, we must each make a willful decision not to love Money. Jesus, in Matthew 6, called Money a god directly in competition with the Creator. If we would find the true value of our lives, according to Ellul, we need to peg our hearts on God's board, and deliberately refuse to be counted on Money's team. This is the implication of James' cryptic words "The brother in humble circumstances ought to take pride in his high position. But the one who is rich should take pride in his low position..."

More than any other advice or admonition this goes against the current of our society. Harvard economist John Kenneth Gailbraith developed the creed of North American life when he declared, as his major economic thesis, "prosperity is generated by desire." If you want to gun for economic greatness you have to feed the flames of greed. Wealth is a perspective on life carved out of insatiable consumer madness.

Ellul's third guideline for defusing the power of money was to give it away. It is not enough, he said, to take God's path at the fork in the road. We must also divest ourselves of the very power of the other god in our lives. Just as alcoholics must renounce the bottle in order to survive, those who are smitten with the plague of greed have to get rid of the things that produce the cancerous disease. Some, in fact, as Jesus noted in the New Testament, may well have to get rid of every bit of money and goods, and take vows of poverty.

Even for those of us who may be able to survive with less drastic healing measures Ellul urges that we all need to give away much more money that is our current habit. Prosperity makes it easy to throw dimes and dollars this way and that without attacking our deep connection to material things. Recession, on the other hand, feeds our worry and robs us of both faith and generosity. To paraphrase the prayer in one of the Proverbs, "Lord, give me neither riches nor poverty; riches will make me self-sufficient and poverty will make me obsessive."

Learning the Grace of Generosity

This is James' point. Precisely when the going gets the toughest the only quality of life that we can bank on is the graciousness of God. That is why the truest test of our spiritual character is found in the reflection of God's generosity that spills out of our souls. As Annie Johnson Flint put it in her hymn:

> **When we have exhausted our store of endurance,**
> **When our strength has failed ere the day is half done,**
> **When we reach the end of our hoarded resources**
> **Our Father's full giving is only begun.**
>
> > **His love has no limit; his grace has no measure,**
> > **His pow'r has no boundaries known unto men;**
> > **For out of his infinite riches in Jesus**
> > **He giveth and giveth and giveth again!**

8

Fade to Black

"...because he will pass away like a wild flower. For the sun rises with scorching heat and withers the plant; its blossom falls and its beauty is destroyed. In the same way, the rich man will fade away even while he goes about his business." (James 1:10-11)

My memories of my great-grandmother Bolt are very vague. I was a young lad when my parents took my older sister and me to see her at a retirement home in Willmar, Minnesota. I can remember the strange and mildly irritating smell of the place, and the dim incandescence of the corridor with its waxed linoleum. We tried unsuccessfully to turn down the volume of our clattering steps and shuffled into the room quietly, nervously afraid of arousing death before its time.

"Grandma Bolt" (as we were told to call her) reclined in an oversized lounger, barely aware of us. Her mouth hung open and she wore wrinkled skin several sizes too big over a shrinking frame. A musty afghan draped her carelessly. She couldn't quite catch what my mom tried to tell her in a stage-whisper shout. We touched her hands and she seemed to fumble for ours with fingers gnarled and cold.

Missing Person

I can only recall this single visit to see her, and I know I didn't like it. At the time she was an alien to me, even though I know now that a good deal of her DNA lives on in my own body. When

Grandma died my parents didn't take me to the funeral because I was supposedly too young to understand death. Now, some forty years later, I weep inside. I never knew the best of my great-grandma Bolt. I wasn't there when she played as a child with boys like me. I never watched her giggle with friends or flirt with my great-grandfather. I never experienced the changing moods of her face, a barometer of her passions and fears and faith. I never heard her sing in church, though I was told she loved the hymns. All I carry with me is the one scary visit of my childhood.

I am old enough now to attend funerals, and I have gotten well past my early aversion to assisted care centers. What frightens me these days is the thought that there are probably fewer than twenty-five people alive today who remember my great-grandmother at all. When we couple dozen die she will be truly forgotten—a near-century of living, breathing, loving, toiling, memorizing, cooking, knitting, talking, aching, laughing, holding, washing, befriending vapored and vanished like a 6 o'clock morning mist.

Nicholas Wolterstorff reflected on the death of his son with these words: "There's a hole in the world now. In the place where he was, there's now just nothing... There's nobody now who saw just what he saw, knows what he knew, remembers what he remembered, loves what he loved... The world is emptier" [*Lament for a Son*, Eerdmans (1987), 33]. That's true, as well, of my great-grandmother Bolt. True, too, of a host of good people whose gravestone legacies weather to indecipherable under time's polishing.

Start Writing the Obituary

And it won't be long before I join them, erased from life's hard drive by the reprogrammers of a new generation. Several weeks ago we were comparing ages in our family and one of my daughters remarked to another, "Dad has probably lived half his life already." The words shivered through me and robbed me of the fun of the moment. It's true—I have probably lived half my life already. In the not-so-distant future I will be my great-grandmother, and only twenty-five minds will retain vague images of a wasted has-been.

In my times of great energy and passionate success I never think about death. I was born to live! I entered this world to conquer! I am a child of greatness, and the stars need do my bidding!

But now and again I see my mortality clinging to my steps like a lengthening shadow, and I am caught wondering why I am here at all. A question chiseled in stone over the grave of a child recycles in my brain: "If I am so quickly done for, what on earth was I begun for?"

James feeds my cynicism. Is he morbid for emphasizing all of this so early in his letter? Perhaps. It may be, however, that he is applying the shock therapy necessary for us to make the most of our run for the roses. Because we are psychosomatic creatures, spirits expressing ourselves through bodies, we often think that the inner self grows in significance as the material self struts with pride and fine fashion. Since no one can touch the soul inside except by way of the material stuff with which we surround it, we are often beguiled into amassing possessions and accomplishments as means to identify our worth.

Weeping Toward Easter

Yet all of these things will be stripped away from us before we can blink against the wind of time. Just today I cried with a thirty-something fellow who is a glowing testimony of success in our community. He grew up in a close-knit family, wears an athletic body and a movie-star's face, married a beautiful and intelligent woman, lives in a luxurious home and is buying a multi-million dollar business that could become a multi-billion dollar corporation before he retires. He was the envy of the neighborhood, but today it means nothing. A crippling disease, a foolish action, and a disintegrating marriage have tripped him on the run. "I would trade everything to have my wife and children back," he said. "Two weeks ago I thought I had it all. Now I don't know if I have anything."

James is not a killjoy. He is perceptive. He knows that God meant for us to live and to enjoy the marvelous beauty and material riches of our world and universe. But he also understands that we can't

31

truly delight in them until we know who we are. It isn't until we begin to die that we begin to live. It isn't until we cry out to heaven that 90 or 75 or 50 or 13 years aren't enough that we begin to understand what 13 or 50 or 75 or 90 years of human life really mean.

If James can whet our appetite for what really matters we will find out that the God who taught our cells to divide in our mothers' wombs won't let the sun set forever. After all, it was James' own brother Jesus who rolled back the stone of death on Easter morning.

9

The Power to See It Through

"Blessed is the man who perseveres under trial, because when he has stood the test, he will receive the crown of life that God has promised to those who love him." (James 1:12)

The world stayed up all night to party at the turn of the millennium. It was a strange event in several ways, if you think about it. For one thing, the dawn of the year 2000 was based on a mistake. About five centuries after Jesus lived, Denis the Small thought it would be good for the world to mark its years from the Messiah's birth. Using available records he managed to make only two mistakes: he missed the year of Jesus' birth by six and he missed the season by about three months. Jesus was probably born in October of what we call 6 B.C., and by better reckoning the year of our Lord (this the meaning of the Latin term "Anno Domine" which we shorten to A.D.) 2000 actually began sometime in the fall of 1994!

A second strange thing about the world party in the wee hours of January 1, 2000, was that cultures all over the globe joined the festivities even though they mark time by vastly different calendars. Only in countries significantly influenced by the Christian religion did time make a millennial move. The most populated nation on earth, China, was in mid-cycle of a vastly different century. Jews and Muslims had no new year or new age to mark that night. A host of other countries and cultures simply ignored their calendars that evening and joined the Christian millennial festivities.

A third odd note about the celebration is that it seems to have resulted more from computer fears than from religious expectations. The electronic data systems of the world faced threats of collapse and sent their shivers through global business and banking. By the time 1999 wound down everyone had stopped to see if the end of civilization would ride a computer glitch. It never occurred, but the mass mania gave people everywhere a reason to jump out of character for a few hours.

Morning Strength

I marveled at the world that millennial night. All wars shut down for a couple days. There was an atmosphere of good will as the party went global. Even the weather seemed to cooperate as God straightened out the jet streams, held back the hurricanes, and blanketed planet earth with settled skies and mild temperatures. It was a promising start to a new age, and I appreciated anew the poet's portrait:

I see the dew glisten as a new day is born

And I hear the birds sing on the wings of the morn

As God wraps up the night and tucks it away

And hands out the sun to herald a new day—

A day yet unblemished by what's gone before,

A chance to begin and start over once more. (Helen Steiner Rice)

There was exuberance in the air that reminded me of Winston Churchill at 75. A photographer was summoned to capture his scowling face on film. Honored to be the one for the job, the cameraman attempted to pay Sir Winston a compliment. "I hope," he said, "that I will be able to shoot your picture on your *hundredth* birthday as well!"

Churchill eyed him closely and finally growled, "I don't see why not, young man; you look reasonably fit and healthy."

Mourning Weakness

34

We should all be so positive about our futures! Yet too well we know how the days and months ahead will sap from us what Harry Emerson Fosdick called "the power to see it through." Rarely do we lose hope and courage in an hour. Instead, our passions leak away over time like a dripping faucet, and we drain our emotional resources a nickel and a dime at a time. Said the poet:

East and west will pinch the heart

That cannot keep them pushed apart;

And he whose soul is flat—the sky

Will cave in on him by and by. (Edna St. Vincent Millay)

Charles Darwin, who grew up in a devoutly Christian home, wrote in his diaries that he never lost his faith through scientific challenge or intellectual argument. Instead, he said, belief slipped away over time until it didn't really matter any more. His story is rewritten a thousand times each generation by others who have simply "lost" faith and felt their souls flatten.

What can broaden and deep and empower our souls enough to help us live lives of significance in this new millennium? Years ago a friend in Israel pointed me to the writings of the great mystic of modern Judaism, Abraham Joshua Heschel. For hours on end I sat in the library of Hebrew University in Jerusalem poring over his sensitive inspiration. Heschel said this: "In the tempestuous ocean of time and toil there are islands of stillness where a man may enter a harbor and reclaim his dignity."

Homecoming Port

Everyone looks at one time or another for places like that, especially those who experience the trials of life that James predicts. Yet where would the tested soul find these islands? Heschel went on: "The Sabbath is the island, the port, the place of detachment from the practical and attachment to the spirit." He pictured us in mad motion: "Rushing hither and thither time becomes soiled and degraded." That's why, he said, we need the Sabbath. It is God's gift, allowing us "the opportunity to cleanse time."

35

The Sabbath is a biblical concept that helps us step out of our own lives in order to see things again from God's perspective. The Sabbath allows us to worship, gaining a harbor for the soul where we can find again our bearings in a sea of lost horizons and wintry winds. This third millennium has begun with great promise, but those who "persevere under trial," as James put it, will likely know well the value of the Sabbath.

10

Desire

"When tempted, no one should say, 'God is tempting me.' For God cannot be tempted by evil, nor does he

tempt anyone; but each one is tempted when, by his own evil desire, he is dragged away and enticed.

Then, after desire has conceived, it gives birth to sin; and sin, when it is full-grown, gives birth to death."

(James 1:13-15)

Lev Tolstoy wrote a brilliant little story about a man who had found favor with the governing powers and was allowed to select a parcel of ground as his own. The only limitation on its size was the requirement that he be able to plow a furrow around the property in a single day.

Early one morning he set out, excited about the small farm he would stake out. He didn't need much—just enough to make a simple living for himself and his family.

Fever

By mid-morning he had moved a great distance. Still, when he looked back the area seemed so small. Since the day was still young he decided to angle out a bit more. After all, a larger farm would make him a wealthy man. In his mind scenes flashed of his children, robust because of their fine meals. He could see his wife gliding at the ball adorned in a Parisian gown. Men would seek his opinions and women would giggle with delight as he tipped his hat to them.

As noon approached the man grew impatient with his slow progress. The circle of land now seemed much too small. He must have more, so once again he widened the angle of his plow.

Throughout the afternoon he fantasized of kings and princes calling him to court, and the fever for more land burned in his soul. He plowed with a passion, forgetting to watch the sun as it slipped in the western skies.

Too late he realized that he might not make it back to the starting stake. In panic he whipped horse, pushing at the plow handles as the furrow began to zigzag madly. His heart pounded, his stomach churned and his muscles tightened in desperation. He *must* make it!

But his desire has overextended itself, and inches short of a complete circle he falls to the earth he covets, dead of a heart attack. He is buried on all the land he needs: a plot of ground three feet by six—a farm for the dead.

Cancer

In his *Ethics* Spinoza said, "Desire is the very essence of man." He was right. The thing that separates us from the instinctive responses of the animal world is the God-given ability to hope and wish and dream and plan. Desire makes us more than mere biological organisms. It is the God-like quality that makes us both loving and creative.

But hidden within every desirable desire in our spirits is the possibility of cancerous mutation. Greed and covetousness are desire gone mad, the degradation of consumerism at its crassest.

In a 15th century morality play the human race is portrayed as a Prince secured within the stronghold of a castle under siege by the Seven Deadly Sins. During the young years of this Prince, Pride, Anger and Sloth inflict many horrible wounds but are not able to gain full access to the castle. As the Prince mirrors an aging humanity most of these Deadly Sins lose their power until six of the seven lie listless outside the fortress gates. Only then does the seventh Deadly Sin, Lust, come to its own. With the battle virtually won, the aging human race opens the doors of the castle and staggers out willingly into the welcoming stranglehold of this final foe.

The lesson is clear: our hearts' desires are our allies in our early years, nourishing the best of God's strength in us. In fact, we are often proud of our strengths, and sometimes mercilessly berate other ages that seemed less competent. But the cancer of consumerism and materialism are already changing our inner selves until, even in our older, seemingly wiser years, the security systems of our hearts fail and we willingly embrace our own ruin in greed.

Prevention

Tolstoy's story of the farmer who died staking his claim was adapted from Jesus' parable of the wealthy landholder who needed to deal with his runaway bumper crop. God called that man "Fool". The judgment against him came not because of his riches but because of the isolation produced by his success. We're told that in his surplus he "took counsel with himself" rather than with his community. That assessment of cancerous desire returns us to James' search for a cure.

When desire becomes cancerous in us, says James, we are "dragged away" from our community and friends. We begin to act as Lone Rangers, isolated and insulated.

The Center for Disease Control in Atlanta has no way to contain the virus, but the church does. When people begin to relearn the value of community in small groups of care and spiritual accountability they can guard one another against desire's cancerous tendencies in the early stages. In my small accountability group we ask each other regularly "Is the public you consistent with the real you?" and "What are you wrestling with in your thought life?" I'm not immune to desires that multiply out of control, and neither are you.

What circle of desire are you plowing around today? You might not be aware of it until it warps you or kills you. Or until your best friends sit across the table from you and help you check your spiritual health. Why not invite them over for coffee today?

11

Illumination

"Don't be deceived, my dear brothers. Every good and perfect gift is from above, coming down from the Father of the heavenly lights, who does not change like shifting shadows." (James 1:16-17)

When I was a radio announcer during my college days our station began a late-night "Contemporary Christian Music" program, one of the first in the nation. We talked about the format for a while, and discussed the content. And, of course, we debated what to call the show.

An early suggestion was "The Solid Rock Hour." Though the double entendre in that title was marvelous ("rock" for the style of some of the music, and "solid rock" as a picture of Jesus Christ), the name itself didn't ring with any contemporary feel. Our final choice was ***ILLUMINATION***, and both the name and the program became a major hit.

Silhouettes

"Illumination" is an interesting term. It speaks of darkness and shadows while at the same time pointing to the growing clarity produced by light and insight. There is a lot of spirituality contained in thoughts of illumination.

It certainly expresses well the God-talk of the Bible: darkness and chaos lurk until God speaks Light and Life; the Psalmist wanders through the Valley of the Shadow of Death with the testimony "The

Lord is my Light and my Salvation" on his lips; Jesus appears as the Light of God entering a dark world; when he hangs on the cross darkness steals the light away and the Shades of Hades appear to take over for a time; yet on Easter morning resurrection comes with the dawn. For these reasons and more John says that "God is Light," and Paul tells us to live as "Children of the Light."

James echoes the same confession here. That doesn't mean, however, that the illumination of God's presence and perspective is immediately apparent to all. It is possible for us to be "deceived," says James, and to live a shadowed existence.

Struggles

C. S. Lewis captured the tension of Light and Darkness in spiritual combat in his space trilogy about Venus. The planet Mars, in his tale, is populated by an ancient race of God's creatures who never gave in to the lure of evil, and remain holy and just. Earth, as we know, has fallen under the domain of the dark shadows, and the Great Creator has posted warning signs around it in space. It is off limits to other races, quarantined until the end of time.

Venus, though, is a new planet with a more recent "Paradise" story of creaturely development. A newly formed pair similar to Earth's Adam and Eve dance about in innocent delight.

The evil power in the universe will not leave a divine masterpiece long unmarred, and he sends a vicious Earth scientist named Weston to introduce sin on Venus by corrupting its Lord and Lady. In a countermove the Great Creator sends an ambassador of his own to Venus. The universe holds its breath as the future of this bright world hangs in the balance.

In these novels Lewis pictured the tension in every human heart. We are surrounded by dark powers, yet long for the light of redemption and love.

Shining in the Dark

One of my friends expresses that struggle in nearly every conversation we have. He grew up in a "religious" home, and was forced to go to church all the time. Yet the message of religion was dark and foreboding. His father ruled with a heavy hand, and the righteousness of the church was ugly, demeaning, and joyless. As soon as my friend was able he left home, got married, started a career, and raised children.

Now he only goes to worship services because his wife thinks that it is important for their children. Yet he is full of anger at his father, and that rage is vented at the church that demanded, scolded, forced and twisted him when he was younger. He shakes his head and his fist at the vengeful and mean-spirited god of his parents' religion.

It has become a problem of identity for my friend. He can never serve the god who dwells in the shadows and cruelly vents meanness and pain. Yet he'll never find the truth of his religion until deception's shadow has been sent packing by the illumination glow of grace "coming down from the Father of heavenly lights, who does not change like shifting shadows."

Most of our lives we struggle to see more clearly. Life gets lost for us, often, in the shadows. But grace breaks through, now and again, in moments of insight and illumination. And those are the moments we have to hang onto.

12

Firstfruits

"He chose to give us birth through the word of truth, that we might be a kind of firstfruits of all he created." (James 1:18)

An ancient Jewish legend declares, "Pentecost is the day on which Torah was given." One wonders whether James might have had that in mind as he penned these words. According to the Jewish teaching it was on the day that eventually became the feast of Pentecost that God gave birth to the Hebrew nation by speaking the divine Covenant to them at Mt. Sinai.

Birthday

As the book of Acts makes clear, Pentecost was the day on which the New Testament church was given birth. Just as God spoke through Moses to bring the nation of Israel into being at Mt. Sinai, so God spoke through Peter to create the first elements of the new faith community.

It was symbolically powerful for these events to take place on Pentecost. In its first use "Pentecost" was essentially a nickname or label. The feast of Passover was one of the most significant holidays in the Jewish community, since it recalled the manner in which God miraculously brought the nation out of Egypt. Seven Sabbaths and a day later ($7 \times 7 + 1 = 50$) the people celebrated this next major religious event as harvest season began in Palestine. Since it occurred fifty days after the Passover people

43

started referring to it as the "Feast after Fifty," or Pentecost.

Yet the real significance of the event was more clearly understood through its original name— Feast of Firstfruits. Regulations for the celebration required all Israelites to assemble at the Temple in Jerusalem bringing with them the first sheaf of grain from their fields. As the time of harvest approached across the land, even before the regular reaping started, a single bundle of grain was cut on each farm and toted off to the Temple.

Testimony

There it was "waved" before the Lord as an offering (Leviticus 23:11) along with two loaves of bread that were baked from the newly harvested grain (Leviticus 23:17). Furthermore, to broaden the impact of the event, two male lambs were also brought from the first castings of each flock (Leviticus 23:12).

As these gifts were presented to God in the Temple courts all of the men danced around the altar that carried the smoke of the gifts toward heaven. The crowds of women, children, and elderly men too old to jump around wildly formed a large circle around these revelers and sang Psalms 113-118. According to historical reports the celebration was often wild and uninhibited.

We might ask what the purpose was behind these religious revelries. The instructions of Moses declared that the feast was a theological testimony. The nation was making a confession that no general harvesting for profit would begin until God had laid claim to the "firstfruits" of the fields and the flocks. By devoting the first of the new produce to God the people were acknowledging that everything came from God and belonged to God. Whatever benefit they might receive from the harvest that year was a direct result of God's care and providential intervention.

Big Plans

With that background the significance of Pentecost as the birthday of the Christian Church takes on new meaning. A new era of God's Kingdom began that day, as God claimed the firstfruits of a worldwide faith harvest. The mission of the Church began only after God had first miraculously owned the original converts from each nation represented in Jerusalem that day.

In that context James speaks of the big plans God has for the world and the church. At the dawn of creation God sowed a world of hope and possibility. Evil storms and tragic seasons may have slowed the harvest of greatness on planet earth. But if anyone wants to know what the true and best harvest will look like, says James, he should check out the church.

That may seem funny to us. We would have a hard time seeing the church as a picture of God's profit margins. Yet for God the church is the firstfruits of the great harvest.

Maybe that's why we ought to take ourselves less seriously and more seriously at the same time, in the church. Less seriously because there is an awful lot of humor in what God is up to. More seriously because God's humor is the first smile of love that the rest of creation around us needs desperately to see.

13

Big Ears, Short Tongue

"My dear brothers, take note of this: Everyone should be quick to listen, slow to speak…" (James 1:19)

At the turn of a new millennium there are many predictions of our future, some promising, some threatening. One prophetic novel describes a coming time in which the world has become an extremely noisy place. In every building a constant hum of conversation buzzes. Surrounding it wafts the ever-present drone of electronic media: talking heads on television monitors, pinging signals, and masking MUSAK. Outside, traffic rumbles. Since world population has exploded, even formerly quiet country haunts are swallowed up in extended rivers of clamorous humanity.

Edited for Broadcast

Enter John. He works at a radio station, editing taped programs. His job is to remove those annoying bits of silence that precede and follow programs. More than that, he must also slice out any gaps that interrupt the constant babble of broadcast voices. By the time John is finished with a tape it shouts with double-digit decibels from one end to the other.

But John is a strange fellow. On the floor of his noisy studio lie strands and snakes of excised tape. It all seems such a waste, so John begins to splice all of those bits and pieces of silence together. Eventually he has produced a reel containing fifteen minutes of quiet nothing.

Every day John plays his silent tape, reclining in a dimly lit room with headphones blocking everything but his inaudible recording. In the stillness John begins to change. He grows annoyed at the daily bombardment of his senses, and becomes addicted to moments when he can crowd his ears with headphones and pause to refresh his soul in the muted nothingness of his lengthening tape of deletions. He starts to resent a chatterbox world in which all is talk and no one really listens.

The Painful Pause

One night John needs to share his quiet revelation, so he invites his girlfriend to his apartment. He tells her he wants her to listen to something, and begins a methodical process of stilling the room. He dims the lights, muffles the relentless television display, and drapes the door and windows with thick pads of foam. His girlfriend is getting nervous at John's strange behavior, and even more agitated with the unaccustomed sensory deprivation. He begs her patience as he threads his precious tape.

"There!" he says as the tape rolls. "Listen to that!"

"To what?" she cries. "I can't hear a thing!"

"I know," replies John with quiet vigor. "Isn't it lovely?"

"Isn't *what* lovely, John? You're scaring me! It's too quiet in here! John, can't we please turn up the television?"

It's a fascinating scene, isn't it? Like something from a Hitchcock movie, or a Ray Bradbury future world, perhaps. Yet, in my experience, it's not as remote as we might wish. I have been in many homes and apartments and offices where the noise never dies. I have tried to carry on pastoral conversations over blaring televisions and radio riots, and I know the cacophony of sleepless city streets.

Learning to Listen

What is more, I know the noise of tongues that wag and mouths forever open. To be a good listener in our age of constant talk is often a dear commodity. I've grown to appreciate deeply those with

47

listening ears. I have also made it a habit and a profession during the past decades to listen to sit quietly with people and encourage them to speak, offering them the privilege of unburdening their souls through the catharsis of confession. I know how hungry most people are to talk, sometimes on and on.

But there are times in my own life when I feel like John, and I need the latitude to be greeted by silence. Some time ago I sat with friends, trying to explain to them the anguish of my soul. I really didn't need a lot of conversation to fill the "dead spots" in our time together. In fact, I hoped to say a few things that were heavy inside, and then sit together with them for a time of subdued thoughtfulness.

Yet every time I allowed a few microseconds of silence to separate my hesitant expressions it seemed as if they needed to interrupt and quickly reply. "Please!" I said to my friends at one point. "I know what you're saying. I understand the wisdom of your advice and I appreciate the suggestions you offer. But please just listen for a few minutes longer! Right now I need, more than anything else, someone who will listen."

My friends were gracious. They not only took my rebuff with kindness; they went on to offer me one of the greatest treasures of deep friendship: the sounds of silence.

14

Pain's Volcano

"Everyone should be... slow to become angry, for man's anger does not bring about the righteous life that God desires." (James 1:19-20)

Anger is like a volcano. Deep inside each of us there is a lake of pain, pure molten hurt. From the outside no one sees it, usually. We cover it over so well. But one day the heat rises, and the dam breaks, and the cork blows, and anger erupts like an explosion. And dogs get kicked. And triggers get pulled. And wives get beaten. And missiles get launched.

Sticks and Stones

There are five levels of pain in our lives. The most obvious is that of physical injury. If someone hits me I hurt, and often I retaliate quickly seeking to share the pain back. It is the rule of the playground, the rule of the hockey ice, the rule of road rage, the rule of international politics. Most of us grow up enough to deal with that pain in more mature ways, but it is always simmering somewhere around us.

The second level of pain is emotional. It is the pain we feel when our security is threatened. Displaced persons and refugees struggle with emotional pain. So do children who bounce around between foster homes: always a new face, a new place, a new space. Every child counselor will speak of the lake of pain that washes around inside these little ones.

49

The third level of pain is social. It is the pain that happens when our closest relationships rub raw. Why do husbands beat their wives? Because no anger is more powerful than the anger we direct toward those we love. Why do family feuds start and fester for years? Because people are bound together in something they cannot escape, and someone will have to pay for the hurt.

Don Posterski and Reginald Bibby interviewed teenagers across North America and found that only 2% said they could talk with their fathers about something critical in their lives. Tony Campolo writes that the most pain he sees as he travels the continent is in the homes of Christians where teens berate parents and parents humiliate teens. The scars of those relationships harden into a cap on the volcano and sometimes keep it from blowing until the next generation arrives. Then is explodes with a vengeance, and the cycle repeats.

Name Calling Hurts Too!

The fourth level of pain is psychological. It is the pain trembling inside when someone attacks our self-esteem. Newspapers carried a horrible story of road rage several years ago: a man was driving through a construction zone where traffic crawled for miles and then funneled into a single lane. For most of an hour the man endured the snail's pace, inching along. Just as the road widened again and traffic began to move another driver bypassed all the stopped cars, bouncing along the shoulder, and pulled in front of this man's vehicle. Not only that—the renegade driver laughed in his face and flipped him the birdie with his finger.

That did it! To be irritated was one thing, but to be taunted and suckered as a fool was quite another. He followed the other car to the next traffic signal. Then he reached into the glove compartment, put out a gun, walked up to the other guy's window and shot him in the face. The psychological pain of humiliation caused the volcano to erupt.

The highest level of pain is rooted in our need for meaning in life. When Simon Wiesenthal was a young Jewish prisoner of war he was led to a room where a Nazi officer lay dying. The injured man said he had to tell Simon a story, and then proceeded to describe a scene of horrible slaughter in which he had personally murdered dozens of Jews in a cruelly painful manner. As the man talked Simon shrank back wondering why he was supposed to hear this.

When the tale ended the Nazi officer announced that he was dying, but that he was scared to enter eternity with this blood on his hands. "Forgive me!" he demands of Wiesenthal. "I need to be forgiven by a Jew!"

What would you do? This man never hurt Simon Wiesenthal personally, physically or emotionally. Yet how can he forgive someone who attacked the very core of his being? Can he forgive this beast and still find any meaning to his life?

Take Another Look

This is pain at its deepest. The molten lake of pain inside bubbles until it fissures in revenge or explodes in rage or seethes in resentment, and hurt strikes out in exasperation.

How can the sources of pain's volcano be discharged before life takes the turns James mentions? For one thing, it has to be identified and acknowledged. Without a finger on pain's pulse we leave it to crouch in wait, a secret snare ready to snap.

Something else needs to happen as well, according to James. The fabric of our lives needs to be reframed by God's grace. Pain happens naturally in our distorted world, and anger hums about hurt. But the frame of grace stretches the scenery in new ways, even if it takes us an eternity to get used to it.

15

"How Does Your Garden Grow?"

"Therefore, get rid of all moral filth and the evil that is so prevalent and humbly accept the word planted in you, which can save you." (James 1:21)

When we were young we chanted poems and what now seem to be nonsense verses:

Seesaw, Marjory Daw, Jack shall have a new master.

He shall have but a penny a day because he can't work any faster.

Or:

One, two, buckle my shoe.

Three, four, close the door.

Five, six, pick up sticks.

Seven, eight, lay them straight.

Nine, ten, a big fat hen.

Or:

Mary, Mary, quite contrary, how does your garden grow?

With silver bells and cockleshells and pretty maids all in a row.

Over the years I've learned bits and pieces of legends that helped shape some of these rhymes. The last one, for instance, seems to have grown out of a disguised accusation about the collecting habits of one of the queens of England. Mary's garden grew an immoral harvest out of her bloody cravings.

You Are What You Eat

Food is a very big part of our lives. Hunger can be a time clock ticking inside, regulating the hours of our days with calculated passion. Or it can be a biologic need, demanding fuel stops on our restless race. Even more, hunger functions as a psychological drive, forcing us to crave chocolate when we lack love, or driving us to drink, drugs and sex.

But deeper than all of these things is our search for meaning beyond the drudgery and repetition of our daily activities. It is the spiritual need each person has to know that she is not alone in this gigantic and sometimes unkind maze of life.

Hunger is what the writer of Ecclesiastes means when he said that God has "set eternity in the hearts of men" (3:11). Hunger is the pilgrimage of the soul. In other words, the old adage is true: "You are what you eat."

So life beckons us to follow the latest fad, to search for the newest fulfillment, to seek the richest treasure. We consume and devour until we are fed up with life, so to speak. And still we want more.

Garbage In, Garbage Out

Then a Word comes to us from heaven. In part it is a Word of judgment against us: since you are what you eat, take a look at what it is that you are consuming. If you eat garbage you become garbage. If you feast on pornography, as Ted Bundy said in his dying confessions to James Dobson, you become filthy. If you think that wealth can satisfy the cravings of your soul you will become a calculator and a penny-pincher. If the adoration of the community feeds the hunger of your psyche you refashion yourself into a code of law and ethics, toeing the line without compassion. If another high is what it takes to get you through the stomach cramps of another day you will shoot up or smoke up or pop some more or tease yourself with illicit sex, and end up becoming a bag of used chemicals and a bottle of cheap thrills.

You are hungry and you are what you eat. The cravings of your soul will not be stilled. A meal will reset the alarm of your biological clock. Food will keep your hungry body going. Potato chips and a soda will stop the munchies for a while. But what are you eating for your soul?

A Richer Harvest

James remembers the beauty and simplicity of what Jesus told people one day: "I am the bread of life. He who comes to me will never go hungry, and he who believes in me will never be thirsty" (John 6:35). Through the symbolic nourishment of spiritual depth and richness something satisfying begins to grow inside. Tasting the things that make heaven shine and earth blossom we begin to find the values and goals and visions and dreams of God giving shape to our lives.

I thought of that when my daughters asked me who knew me better than anyone else in life. They suggested several possibilities: my colleagues at work, my parents, my friends. All along, of course, they knew that it was their mother, my wife, who knew me best. Yet *how* did she know me so well, they asked. As we probed the matter further we finally agreed that it had to be by my actions and attitudes toward her. Whatever lives in me eventually comes out from me in words and deeds and perspectives. I cannot hide long what grows powerfully inside.

Augustine knew this as he reflected on the spiritual character of our race. "Man is one of your creatures, Lord," he said, "and his instinct is to praise you. The thought of you stirs him so deeply that he cannot be content unless he praises you, because you made us for yourself and our hearts find no peace until they rest in you."

What are you eating today? Tomorrow and next week those who are close to you will know whether there was any eternal nourishment in your diet.

16

Beyond Sophisticated Indifference

"Do not merely listen to the word, and so deceive yourselves. Do what it says!" (James 1:22)

When Mahatma Gandhi traveled from his India homeland as a young man, and studied for a time in England, he was curious about the religion of the British people. To learn more he bought a Bible and began to read it. He was amazed—this was good stuff! Jesus' Sermon on the Mount (Matthew 5-7) particularly intrigued him. This was a view of life that really made sense! Surely the Christian faith was a religion of great significance!

The Yawning Gap

The next Sunday Gandhi dressed early for a visit to a nearby church. He wasn't sure what would take place in a Christian worship service, but he knew that he wanted to be part of it. According to his testimony, he had decided already that he wanted to become a Christian.

Unfortunately that worship service was one of the most awful events of his life. The singing was half-hearted; many people just stood with mouths closed or merely mumbled along in boredom. The sermon was a tedious explanation of some fine point of doctrine. It said so little, and took so long to say it. Gandhi was glad to see that at least some people benefited from the service—they slept through most of it.

Gandhi tried to be a fair person, so the next Sunday he went to a worship service at another church. He hoped, expectantly, for some of the power and significance that breathed through the Bible. Yet this congregation was little different from the last. The atmosphere among the people was that of sophisticated indifference, and Gandhi left with an empty heart. He tried a number of different churches for the next three months but never met more than a kind of middle-class churchianity.

Gandhi decided that the Christian church has nothing of value for him, and he returned to his Hindu religious practices. To his dying day, however, he continued to read Jesus' Sermon on the Mount. He also carried on a life-long discussion with certain Christian leaders as to why their religion, built on such a magnificent foundation, seemed to make so little difference in people's lives.

Rescue Brigade

How does the power go out of our religion and turn Christianity into complacent indifference? Someone once described the process in allegorical terms.

There was a small community living along a rocky seacoast, he said. The shoreline was treacherous, and not a few ships foundered and crashed there on the rocks and reefs.

But the town had a caring disposition and the people formed a Rescue Brigade to respond quickly to navigational disasters. Every time a ship crashed they sounded the alarm and raced to help those wrestling against hope in the waves. Sometimes a little cargo was rescued, and maybe a sailor or two. But most times the wreck was a total loss, and everyone on shore grieved.

The people of the community wanted to do more. They wanted to prevent the disasters from happening, so they organized a Fire Brigade. By day the Fire Brigade gathered wood from the forest, and every night they lit a fire that served to warn the ships at sea. Because of the signal fire tended every night by the Fire Brigade fewer ships crashed and more lives were saved.

At the start everybody wanted to be a member of the Fire Brigade. After all, most of them had first come to the community through disasters at sea. They had been drawn from the wreckage by other hands, and now they wanted to do the same for those who were still at sea.

The Fall of the Lighthouse Brigade

But the work was hard, and most of it was volunteer. The nights were long, and when it rained or stormed it was tough to take a turn at the post. After a while the Fire Brigade subtly began to change. First, some charter members of the Fire Brigade started hiring others to do the work for them, particularly during the snows of winter. Next, the leaders of the Brigade instituted a tax on all goods rescued from the sea. Out of these funds a warming house was erected, where members of the Fire Brigade could sleep and eat in comfort.

Soon it was decided that fires at night were much too inefficient. A tower was raised, and a kerosene lamp at the top that shone far out to sea.

Of course, nobody had to gather wood anymore, or tend the fires. The warming house became a meeting hall. Soon it was such a popular place to hold parties and dances that the community expanded it, adding rooms and catering services.

The old Fire Brigade renamed itself the Lighthouse Brigade and was the center of social life for miles around. A social coordinator and administrative team were hired to manage the Lighthouse Group Properties. Others were brought in to plan the parties and develop corporate structures.

One night a terrific storm blew in. The light in the tower was extinguished by the gusts. Nobody noticed in the luxurious Lighthouse Club Hall below. The music and dancing went on.

Three ships crashed on the rocks that night, and thousands of lives were lost. But the people of the Lighthouse Brigade never knew. And they didn't care.

17

Spiritual Alzheimer's

"Anyone who listens to the word but does not do what it says is like a man who looks at his face in a mirror and, after looking at himself, goes away and immediately forgets what he looks like." (James 1:23-24)

A few years back I got a package in the mail wrapped in brown paper and sporting an unknown address written in an unfamiliar hand. When I tore it open I found a book that used to be a favorite of mine. So many times I had looked through my bookshelves for it, and for these last years it had eluded me. I thought there must be another box of books stashed somewhere in our basement from one of our moves, and it was still hiding from me.

Now it was in my hands again, along with notes I had taken for a philosophy course at college. A note solved the mystery. One of my college buddies had borrowed the book and notes from me long ago and only recently, during one of his moves, discovered them. His apology was profuse.

Books have a way of wandering. I went back to a former congregation to preach one Sunday and found a stack of eleven books with my name in them on the table in the room where we were to meet for pre-service prayer. No one ever told me who put them there, but several encouraged me to take them home with me. Another time I was visiting with a widow whose husband had been a great friend of mine years before. She pulled out a book and said, "I found this in John's things and thought you might want to have it back." Although I'm glad to have the book again, I wish I could have John instead.

The Good, the Bad, and the Missing

Missing books have been a malady of readers throughout the ages. Sir Walter Scott of several centuries ago feared to lend his books to even the best among his friends. If someone begged him long enough he might hand it over. But he always gave each borrower very specific instructions about how he had to care for the book and when he had to bring it back. Someone asked him why he made such a deal about it and he replied, "Although my friends are very bad at arithmetic, they tend to be very excellent at bookkeeping.

He put his finger on one of the great weakness of humankind—forgetfulness. The saying carries much truth: "Out of sight, out of mind." In fact, the most pervasive new year's resolution in ancient Babylon was a desire to return borrowed tools and utensils to their rightful owners.

Sometimes, of course, forgetfulness can be a good thing. God has blessed us with the ability to remember the best in life while often forgetting the severity of pain and suffering. Mothers quickly forget the pain of childbirth as they celebrate new life. Children wonder about their grandparents' selective memories when hearing stories about the "good ol' days"—everything then was bigger, taller, further, harder, better, or more magnificent than any dull thing today! What a fantasyland the past must have been, and how boring the world has become!

Forgetfulness feeds the optimism of our hope. One poet suggested well:

Always remember to forget the things that made you sad;

But never forget to remember the things that made you glad.

If our forgetfulness helps us keep a positive and thankful outlook on life it serves us well. Sometimes, though forgetfulness can be embarrassing. I've walked up to people I know and completely lost their names. Last week I was teaching a Bible class and some of the most basic parts of the lesson slipped my mind completely. Today I remembered a name I wanted to mention to a colleague I was meeting—only I remembered the name three hours after my friend and I had parted ways.

A Nasty Disease

As Ralph Waldo Emerson grew older he had problems with his memory. He said it played tricks on him, hiding words behind screens in his mind at all the wrong moments. When he went to a funeral for a dear, life-long friend, he was asked to say a few words of eulogy. Standing before other friends and family he stumbled about for a few moments and then said, "That gentleman had a sweet, beautiful soul, but I have entirely forgotten his name." How embarrassing and tragic!

Sometimes our forgetfulness can be more than embarrassing; it can be downright sinful. During a low period in the economy butcher William Webb of West Worthing, Saskatchewan, was near bankruptcy. Although he had carried on a good business many of his customers suddenly developed urgent cases of amnesia and forget to pay their accounts. In desperation Webb posted a sign in his shop window: THIS BUSINESS HAS BEEN COMPELLED TO CLOSE OWING TO BAD DEBTS. A LIST OF NAMES AND AMOUNTS OWING WILL SHORTLY BE SHOWN.

Amazingly, within hours the haze cleared in many minds around the community and forgotten debts were paid up. Webb was able to stay in business and ride out the recession.

James seems to have something like that in mind when he calls us out of our typical bouts of spiritual Alzheimer's disease. Forgetfulness may be cute sometimes, but when we forget who we are before God the results can be tragic.

18

Bound Free

"But the man who looks intently into the perfect law that gives freedom, and continues to do this, not forgetting what he has heard, but doing it – he will be blessed in what he does." (James 1:25)

John Hull's autobiography, *Touching the Rock*, is both a personal story and a spiritual saga. At the age of 17, John began to go blind in his left eye. One day he realized that the only way he would ever see his left shoulder again would be by turning to his side and catching his reflection in the mirror with his right eye. Later the blindness spread and John's sight was gone entirely.

Between Faces

John writes that for a while he tried to remember what he looked like. He thought about old photographs of himself, and struggled to recall what he used to look like when he shaved. After a while, though, his memory banks gave out and he couldn't remember his own face anymore.

"Who am I?" he thought, with a wash of panic. "If I don't even know my own face, who am I?"

Worse still was his daughter Lizzie's question. She was only four years old when she asked him, "Daddy, how can a smile be between us when you can't see my face?"

It was Lizzie's curious questions that prompted John Hull to write his book. As he surveyed his life in its spiritual dimension he took her query a level higher. "How can a smile be between us and God if we cannot see *his* face?" John asked.

An Indistinct Mirror

John finally reflected that the only way it can happen is when we take what little God gives us to work with and use it as a kind of tarnished mirror to seek out God's distant face. In other words, said John, the scriptures and the person of Jesus help us take first steps toward making a smile happen between ourselves and God. In this he echoed James' reflection that we find ourselves at our best when we spend time in front of the mirror of scripture.

Generations ago the English poet George Herbert penned a brilliant picture of the near-phantom connection that links us to God. In "The Pulley" he portrayed God at the moment of creation, sprinkling his new human creature with treasures kept in a jar beside him. These were God's finest resources, given now as gifts to the crown of his universe: beauty, wisdom, honor, pleasure… All were scattered liberally in the genetic recipe of our kind.

When the jar of God's treasures was nearly empty, God put the lid on it. The angels wondered why God did not finish the human concoction, leaving one great resource still in its container. This last quality, God told the angels, is "rest." But God would not grant that divine treasure to the human race.

Restless Spirituality

The angels, of course, asked why. Herbert was ready with the divine answer regarding the best mix for the human spirit:

> **Let him be rich and weary, that at least,**
>
> **If goodness lead him not, yet weariness**
>
> **May toss him to my breast.**

Herbert saw well that the strong talents and marvelous abilities of humankind would make us like impatient children, eager to strike out on our own and find our self-made destinies. Only if God would hold back a sense of full satisfaction from our souls would we search our way back home. James expresses the same idea in what remains a perennial theological paradox: it is the law of God that gives freedom. When we use our abilities for our own ends we tend to destroy what is best in ourselves and others. When, however, we are restless to find the face of God in the divine law's mirror we find a glimpse of our own best faces reflected back toward us in smile of God's.

George Matheson, the blind hymn writer, gave the same prayer to the church when he wrote:

Make me a captive, Lord, and then I shall be free.

Force me to render up my sword and I shall conqueror be.

I sink in life's alarms when by myself I stand;

Imprison me within Thine arms and strong shall be my hand.

> **My will is not my own 'til Thou hast made it Thine.**
>
> **If it would reach a monarch's throne it must its crown resign.**
>
> **I only stand unbent amid the clashing strife**
>
> **When on Thy bosom I have leaned and found in Thee my life.**

19

Whoa, Tongue!

"If anyone considers himself religious and yet does not keep a tight rein on his tongue, he deceives himself and his religion is worthless." (James 1:26)

When Ernest Hemmingway was testing his writing skills at the start of his journalistic career, communicating did not come easily for him. He was frustrated that while words seemed to tumble onto paper almost by themselves from his pen, meanings were so hard to get at. One day in Paris an insight flashed through his mind. The key to good writing, he realized, "is simply writing stuff that is true."

Yet merely writing something that is true proved more difficult than he had imagined. From that morning in January when the inspiration flared Hemingway began every day to write what he termed one single, authentic, true and personal declarative sentence. By the end of May, five months later, he had managed to construct six straightforward true sentences. Only then, according to his biographer Carlos Baker, was Hemingway on his way to becoming a writer.

Selling Ourselves

Perhaps Hemingway struggled with deeper issues of communication than most of us will have to face. Still, his is a worthy recognition that talk is often cheap. Words can just as easily mislead as they can instruct. As a pastor who listens to many people converse I know how easily we can hide behind words;

as a wordsmith of sorts myself I know the danger of words that paint false pictures. Philip Yancey once told a large audience that it is very possible for an author to disguise himself behind the written page even while readers are sending him notes on how transparent and vulnerable he is with them.

Psychiatrist Wood Hill identified five personality types that are particularly prone to twisting and stretching the truth. The narcissist, said Dr. Hill, lies to impress himself and others of his magnificence of character or accomplishment. A narcissistic mother manages to make every conversation a platform for declaiming her wonderful children who are obviously much more beautiful and handsome and brilliant than yours. A narcissistic manager tells you his boss thinks he is the next CEO of the company. Truth is never true unless it is embellished.

A second deceptive character type is the compulsive personality, according to Dr. Hill. Compulsive people try to be honest, he says, but because they are often great sticklers for perfection they won't admit to finishing anything. For that reason life becomes a lengthy (and, as far as others are concerned, an unnecessary) apology, disguising anything good they might have done as something significantly less.

Warped Reality

Dr. Hill next identifies the hysteric personality. For these people there is an excessive need to be noticed or affirmed or encouraged. To trigger that response in others they create new "truths" on the run, hoping to bind people to them in sympathy or catharsis. The common greeting "Hi! How are you today?" will call out a litany of disease and disorder symptoms no one could have diagnosed a few moments earlier.

Fourth are what Dr. Hill describes as "borderline" personalities. These people tend to be impulsive and reckless because they have difficulty tolerating frustration. Their dangerous or inappropriate actions get them into trouble. Yet, unable to accept responsibility for their actions, these borderline personalities quickly shift the blame to others. It is a childlike response become childish in adults. Boundaries are crossed, people get hurt and things are destroyed. Before long friends become accusers and "truth" goes through a number of fascinating metamorphoses.

The fifth group in Dr. Hill's analysis are truly antisocial persons, people whose sense of moral value has been compromised severely. Selfish motives drive them to callous and calculated lies. Another psychiatrist, M. Scott Peck, in fact, called these folks *People of the Lie* (Simon & Schuster, 1983), and explored the manner in which they live out the description Jesus gave in John's gospel.

Catching the Reverb

While all of this is interesting as I observe people around me, the real issue as I read James' exhortation is that I see a little of myself in each of these personality types. I know how much I want to impress people. I agonize to do things right, sometimes insecurely becoming self-deprecating and untrue in the process. At times I just want people to care about me when I hurt, so I'll pull at heartstrings to get attention. I don't like to be at fault, and there are times when I will point fingers everywhere but at my own heart. I even have to admit that occasionally I can be cruel and calculating, using partial truths to warp reality.

I know why James says that talk is cheap. A fine testimony can be a dime a dozen. The disease of falsehood is far more pervasive than cancer or AIDS. We all need a doctor. But sometimes we won't admit it until we shut up and for a while and listen to ourselves.

20

What Kind of Church Do You Belong To?

"Religion that God our Father accepts as pure and faultless is this: to look after orphans and widows in their distress..." (James 1:27)

When Tony Campolo spoke at a conference in Hawaii it took a while for his body to catch up with the move across five time zones. The first night at his hotel his internal clock buzzed at 3 a.m. and his stomach growled for attention.

Tony wandered quiet Honolulu streets looking for a place to get fried eggs and bacon. All the respectable places were closed, and Tony finally ended up at a greasy dive in a narrow and dim alley. The place reeked with grunge. Tony was afraid to touch the menu for fear that it would stick to his fingers and that if he opened it something with too many legs to count might crawl out.

The guy behind the counter growled at him. "What d'ya want?"

Suddenly Tony wasn't hungry, no matter how much his stomach protested. He saw a stack of donuts under a cracked plastic cover. "I'll have a donut and a coffee," he said. That ought to be safe.

The guy poured a cup of dark, thick coffee. Then he wiped his greasy hand on his dirty apron, grabbed a donut with his fingers and threw it on the counter in front of Tony. There sat Tony Campolo at 3:30 in the morning, gagging on sour coffee and a stale donut.

Strange Neighborhood

All at once the door slammed open and eight or nine prostitutes sauntered in, just finished with a night's work. The joint was small and when the women crowded at the counter they surrounded Tony, swearing, smoking and gossiping tales of their Johns. Another gulp and bite, and Tony would scram.

But something stopped his exit when the woman next to him turned to her friend and said, with a faraway look in her eye, "You know what? Tomorrow's my birthday. I'm gonna be thirty-nine…"

The other woman got nasty. "So what d'ya want from me?" she said. "A birthday party? Ya want me to get you a cake that says 'Happy Birthday' on it?"

The first woman whimpered a bit and replied, "Awe, come on! Why do ya have to be so mean? I was just tellin' you, that's all. You do ya have to put me down? I don't want anything from you! I mean, why should you give me a birthday party? I've never had a birthday party in my whole life! Why should I have one now?"

That got Tony thinking. He stayed until the women left, then said to the fellow behind the counter, "Do they come in here every night?"

"Yep," said the man. "Every night."

Tony asked him if he knew the one who sat next to him. "Sure, that's Agnes. She's been coming here for years. Comes every night about this time."

Party Time

"Well," said Tony, "she just said that it was her birthday tomorrow. What do you think? You think you and I could do something about that—maybe throw her a birthday party right here tomorrow night?"

The man got a cute smile on his chubby cheeks. "That's great!" he said. He turned to the window at the kitchen and shouted to his wife who was doing the cooking, "Hey, come out here! This guy's got a great idea. Tomorrow's Agnes' birthday, and this guy wants us to go in with him and throw a party for her right here tomorrow night!"

His wife appears from the back. "That's wonderful," she says. "You know, Agnes is really a nice person. She's always trying to help other people. And nobody ever does anything nice for her."

So they made their plans. Tony would be back at 2:30 the next morning. He said he would help decorate the place and bring a birthday cake. "No way!" retorted the man. "My name's Harry, and this is my place, and around here I make the cakes!"

At 2:30 the next morning Tony was back. He brought crepe paper decorations and a fold-out sign that said **HAPPY BIRTHDAY AGNES!** By 3 o'clock the diner was looking pretty good. By 3:15 it was crowded with wall-to-wall prostitutes. Harry's wife had gotten the word out on the streets and every Honolulu streetwalker showed up.

At 3:30 Agnes and her group walked in. Tony had everyone ready for a shout, "Happy birthday, Agnes!" She was flabbergasted. Her mouth fell open, her legs wobbled, she put her hands to her head and almost fell over stunned. Her friend grabbed her by the arm and led her to the counter where her birthday cake rested on a pedestal. Tony led the room in an energetic chorus of "Happy Birthday to You."

Agnes began to cry. She saw the cake with all the candles and wept. Harry, who was not used to seeing a prostitute cry, said rather gruffly, "Blow out the candles, Agnes! Come on! Blow out the candles! If you don't blow 'em out, I'll have to do it!"

So Agnes composed herself, and after a minute or two she blew them out. Everyone cheered. "Cut the cake, Agnes," they yelled. "Cut the cake!"

But Agnes looked down at the cake and, without taking her eyes off it, said to Harry, "Look, Harry... Would it be all right with you if I... I mean, is it okay if I... What I mean is, do you think it's be okay if I just *kept* the cake for a little while? I mean, is it all right if we don't eat it right away?"

Harry didn't know what to say. He shrugged his shoulders and said, "Sure, if that's what you want. Go ahead and keep the cake. Take it home if you want to."

Agnes turned to Tony and asked again, "Is it okay? I live just down the street. Can I take the cake home for a minute? I'll be right back. Honest!"

Street Religion

Agnes picked up the cake like it was the Holy Grail itself. Slowly she promenaded through the room with it high in front of her for everyone to see. She carried her treasure out the door and everyone there watched her in stunned silence. When she was gone nobody seemed to know what to do, so Tony got up on a chair and said, "What do you say we pray."

There they were together in a hole-in-the-wall greasy spoon, all the prostitutes of Honolulu's streets, at 3:30 in the morning, and Tony gathered them to pray for Agnes. He prayed for her life. He prayed for her health. He prayed for her soul and her relationship with God.

When Tony finished praying Harry leaned over the counter and said, accusingly, "Hey! You never told me you was a preacher! What kind of a church do you belong to anyway?"

Tony replied, "I belong to a church that throws parties for prostitutes at 3:30 in the morning."

Harry thought about that for a moment and then said, "Naw you don't! There ain't no church like that! If there was, I'd join it! Yessir, I'd be a member of a church like that!"

21

The Deeper Identity

"Religion that God our Father accepts as pure and faultless is this… to keep oneself from being polluted by the world." (James 1:27)

Some years ago a major research firm conducted a survey to determine what people would be willing to do for $10 million. The results were astounding. 3% would put their children up for adoption. 7% would kill a stranger. 10% would lie in court to set a murderer free. 16% would divorce their spouses. 23% said they would become prostitutes for a week or longer.

Most astonishing was the category at the top of the list. One-fourth of all surveyed said that they would leave their families for $10 million.

Everyone has a selling price at which he or she will step over a line of conduct and allow someone else to dictate the terms of behavior. It might be $10 million or it might only be one more bottle of wine. It might be a night in the spotlight or a night in bed. In Shusaku Endo's powerful novel *Silence*, the missionary priest Rodriguez steps over the line when torture exceeds what his soul can bear, and he desecrates an image of Jesus. We all have our selling price.

The Self We Receive

Our selling price is linked to our identity. The stronger our sense of who we are the higher our selling price and the deeper our character. There are, however, several identities that each of us wears.

The first is the identity we receive from others. We get our looks and temperament from our parents. We garner our tastes and styles from our culture. There is even something mystical about us that we receive as a gift from God, unique to our personalities. Paul talks at length about these spiritual gifts in 1 Corinthians 12-14.

Poet John Masefield understood that when he reflected on how it was that he started writing and rhyming. One day he picked up a volume of Geoffrey Chaucer's works and was gripped by the art of the lines. Masefield couldn't put the book down. That night he read until a whole new world opened for him. By the time morning broke, said Masefield, he had finished the entire book, set it down, looked at the dawning day and quietly said, "I too am a poet." And so he was.

The Self We Make

A second identity we have in life is the one we make. In the drama *The Rainmaker* the main character is a con artist who calls himself Starbuck. He travels from town to town during the Dirty 30's scheming to get people to pay him to bring the rains for their parched fields.

Young Lizzie Curry catches his eye and they spar with building passion. But Lizzie is no fool and she challenges him to come clean with her about his true name. It can't really be Starbuck, she knows.

Starbuck admits that he was born a "Smith," but asks, "What kind of name is that for a fellow like me? I needed a name that had the whole sky in it! And the power of a man! Starbuck! Now there's a name—and it's mine!"

Lizzie tries to contradict him, telling him he has no right choosing his own name and giving up his family heritage. Yet he will not capitulate quickly. "You're wrong, Lizzie," he says. "The name you choose for yourself is more your own name than the name you were born with!"

Starbuck is on to something. Much of what we see in people around is has to do with what they have made of themselves. When an English nobleman named Roberts was having his portrait painted the artist asked him if he would like the lines and creases in his face smoothed over.

"Certainly not!" he objected. "Make sure you put them all in. I earned every single wrinkle on my face!"

He was a man who knew the identity he had made.

The Self that Makes Us

There is also a third and deeper human identity. It is the identity that transforms us from what we were to what we are becoming. The poet saw a friend clearly when he wrote:

> **And there were three men went down the road**
>
> **As down the road went he:**
>
> **The man they saw, the man he was,**
>
> **And the man he wanted to be.**

The person we each want to be when we find our truest selves in God is larger than either the identity we have received from others or the one we try to create. This is the thought James hopes to encourage in his cryptic definition of religion. Anything that sullies us by trying to define us on terms less than God's grace limits our best self.

Someone has suggested a powerfully illuminating analogy. When a ship is built, he said, each part has a little voice of its own. As seamen walk the passageways on her maiden voyage they can hear the creaking whispers of separate identities: "I'm a rivet!" "I'm a sheet of steel!" "I'm a propeller!" "I'm a beam!" For a while these little voices sing their individual songs, proudly independent and fiercely self-protective.

But then a storm blows in on the high seas and the waves toss, the gales hurl, and the rain beat. If the parts of the ship try to withstand the pummeling independent from one another each would be lost. On

73

the bridge, however, stands the Captain. He issues orders that take all of the little voices and bring them together for a larger purpose. By the time the vessel has weathered the storm sailors hear a new and deeper song echoing from stem to stern: "I am a ship!"

It is the Captain's call that creates the deeper identity. So too in our lives, according to James. Minor stars in a world of glamour try to sing Siren songs pulling bits and pieces of us from the voyage of our lives. Those who hear the Captain's call are able to sail true and straight.

22

Favoritism

"My brothers, as believers in our glorious Lord Jesus Christ, don't show favoritism. Suppose a man comes into your meeting wearing a gold ring and fine clothes, and a poor man in shabby clothes also comes in. If you show special attention to the man wearing fine clothes and say, "Here's a good seat for you," but say to the poor man, "You stand there" or "Sit on the floor by my feet," have you not discriminated among yourselves and become judges with evil thoughts?" (James 2:1-4)

Norwegian playwright Henrik Ibsen was traveling in Rome when he noticed a crowd of people gathered around a large red poster. They were talking rather animatedly among themselves about the message it announced, and Ibsen was curious to know what was causing the commotion. When he reached into his coat pocket, however, he realized that he'd left his eyeglasses back at his hotel. Not wanting to be left out of the excitement, he turned to the fellow next to him and said, "Signore, could you please tell me what that sign says? I've forgotten my glasses."

The man turned toward him with a "knowing" look in his eyes and replied, "Sorry, Signore, but I don't know how to read either!"

Eye Exam

As with Ibsen, glasses are a necessary evil for me. I can't get along without them. If I take my glasses off, I can't see anything clearly further than   about 8 inches in front of my nose! As I was getting into bed on a night many years ago, one of our daughters (very young at the time) saw me take off my glasses. She thought that was a wonderful thing for me because then I wouldn't have any bad dreams---I couldn't (in her logic) see the monsters in my nightmares!

Corrective eyewear is a physical necessity for many of us. But James says that corrective eyewear is also a spiritual necessity for our hearts. As Dr. Karl Menninger once put it, "Attitudes are more important than facts." For that reason James indicates a trip to the "glorious" light of Jesus Christ is part of a spiritual ophthalmologist exam. Once we enter the light of Christ we need glasses that will change our attitudes about each other. We need glasses of the heart that will alter our perceptions. We need corrective lenses of the soul that will make us encourage and build others up, rather than cut them down.

Story of a "Loser"

Johan Eriksson learned that lesson well. In 1939 trainloads of Jewish children were piling into Sweden. Because of the changing political climate under Hitler's European campaign, parents were trying to get their young ones out of Germany. Boys and girls, sometimes only three or four years old, stumbled off boxcars and into culture shock carrying nothing but large tags around each neck, announcing their names, ages, and hometowns.

The Swedes had agreed to take in the children "for the duration of the war." Unfortunately there were more children than suitable homes, so even Johan Eriksson was called. Johan was a widower, middle-aged and gruff, and not a likely candidate for foster parenting.

Without comprehending why, young Rolf walked away from the train station next to Johan. The boy was starving at the time, and frightened into silence. Every time he heard a noise at Johan's door, little Rolf would run into a closet and pull coats over his head.

For years Rolf wouldn't smile. He hardly ate. Johan created a Spartan but stable home for Rolf, biding his time until Rolf would be gone and he could get back to his life. Yet Rolf never went back to Germany because no one ever sent for him. His parents perished in the ovens.

76

So Johan did his best with a son he never anticipated. When Rolf was in his twenties, Johan managed to get him a job in Stockholm. For a while Rolf struggled along, but he couldn't handle the pressures. "His mind just snapped one day," his employer said, and the local authorities wanted to put him in a mental institution.

Seeing Beyond Seeing

Johan set out immediately to rescue his boy. Johan was an old man now, yet he brought Rolf home again to the little city of Amal. For many years Johan nursed Rolf back to health.

Rolf finally got better. He married a wonderful woman. He established a fairly successful business, and even became quite wealthy. All along, though, he knew that his achievements were only possible because of Johan, the big Swede, who took in a nobody, loved him back to life, gave him an identity and hugged away his fears.

When doctors called Johan's children home for a final parting in his dying days, Rolf was the first to arrive. From an orphan's tragedy, his life had become the story of a dearly loved son.

Johan was a Christian. He found the spiritual corrective eyewear that James prescribes. It gave him the ability to see little Rolf as God saw him, and Rolf began to live that day.

Said Mark Twain, "You can't depend on your eyes when your imagination is out of focus." True! But when you get that new pair of eyeglasses for your soul, everything begins to look different. James would say that it has to do with the light of "our glorious Lord Jesus Christ" restoring in us the true ability to see.

23

Sticker Prices

"Listen, my dear brothers: Has not God chosen those who are poor in the eyes of the world to be rich in faith and to inherit the kingdom he promised those who love him?" (James 2:5)

Soren Kierkegaard once wrote of a strange break-in at a large store in his native Denmark where the thieves didn't remove anything. When clerks opened up in the morning, all the merchandise was still there. Instead of stealing the goods, the thieves had stolen value. They had switched all the price tags, so that the worth of each item had no relation to its price: a diamond necklace valued at $2; a pair of leather shoes for 50 cents; a pencil selling for $75, and a baby's rattle with $5000 on the sticker.

Altered States

Sometimes it seems as if our society has been invaded by thieves like that. Just when we think we know the value of something the sticker price begins to spin. Worse still, the values placed on us can bounce like a stock market chart until we don't know who we are anymore.

Shelley Rodriguez remembers the time she brought her grandson to a farm sale near their home in Independence, Kentucky. The boy was 8 years old at the time. Immediately he was captured by the magic of the auctioneer's sing-song voice. Yet something bothered him.

"Grandma," he asked, "how is that man ever going to sell anything if he keeps changing the prices?"

That's a good question for all of us.

Tear on the Dotted Lines

Of course, one might also wonder about God's price tags of human worth when reading these words of James. Why should "those who are poor in the eyes of the world" have a higher value in heaven's gaze than any other demographic group?

Though the answer is always a little slippery, James' assertion seems to have to do with the complexity of the human spirit. The hardest thing for any of us to do in life is to maintain integrity. Even though we are not, most of us, evil people, sin has a way of playing around with our hearts. On the outside we appear rather nice and respectable. In fact, much of we do is good and noble and kind and wise. No one can deny that.

The problem is that sin has a way slicing our hearts with perforated lines. Before we are aware of it we have torn off a piece here and a section there, till we find ourselves segmented. Fragmented. Torn apart in separate snippets of self.

It isn't that we become blackened by sin in large strokes. Nor do we generally turn into some hideous monsters of greed and cruelty, dissolving the kind Dr. Jekyll's of our personalities into dastardly Mr. Hyde's. Instead, we keep most of our goodness intact while making small allowances in certain little areas. We shave our taxable income as we fill out our 1040s, maybe. Or we lose our peripheral vision when someone in need approaches. Or we compromise our communication so that we speak from only our mouths but not our souls.

The fragmentation of our lives makes us less than we should or could be. We strut on tiny legs, ants marching across the busy highway of life imagining that tires of destruction will skid around us.

79

Slippery Selves

In Robert Bolt's play *A Man for All Seasons* Sir Thomas More stands at a moral crossroads. More has been a loyal subject of the English crown, supporting his king in both civil and ecclesiastical matters. Now, however, King Henry VIII is engaged in a devious plan that pits his own desires against that of the church. In order to pull off his scheme Henry requires that all his nobles to swear to him a personal oath of allegiance. Because the terms of the oath violate More's conscience before his God, he refused and is arrested and jailed.

More's daughter Margaret comes to visit him. She is his pride and joy, often thinking his thoughts after him. In their playful terms of endearment she is her father's "Meg," and Henry knows that More will do anything for her. That's why he sent Meg to plead with her father in prison. "Take the oath, Father!" she urges him. "Take it with your mouth, if you can't take it with your heart! Take it and return to us! You can't do us any good in here!"

In so many ways she's right, of course—how can More bless and protect his family if he rots in jail or dances with the executioner? And who will know if More coughs a testimony he doesn't fully believe?

Sir Thomas, however, has felt the creases in his heart and knows what will happen to him if he finds himself rather than King Henry the betrayer in the mirror. So he says, "Meg, when a man swears an oath, he holds himself in his hands like water. And if he opens his fingers, how can he hope to find himself again?"

When our lives begin to fragment, as Thomas More knew, we are left like holding our lives as water in our hands. As the cracks between our fingers shift, even slightly, the water of our very selves dribbles away. We may look like the same people, but who we are inside has begun to change.

That is why those whom James calls "poor in the eyes of the world" are often misunderstood. Integrity, when it happens, seems to make people so simple. What you see is what you get.

Maybe, though, that is when sticker prices finally make sense.

24

Beyond Prejudice

"But you have insulted the poor." (James 2:6)

The great composer Felix Mendelssohn loved to tell the marvelous story of how his grandparents Moses and Frumte Mendelssohn met and married. Moses was very short and far from handsome. He walked with a limping gate, partly because he sported a very noticeable hunch back.

The day Moses met Frumte Cupid's arrow struck deep. He determined to win the hand of this young beauty, the daughter of a local businessman. He knew it would be difficult because, like other young women of Hamburg, Frumte was repulsed by his misshapen body. Only after Moses made many requests to her father did she reluctantly agree to see him.

Sleepless in Hamburg

Frumte did not fall in love with Moses, however. At the same time, in spite of her constant resistance, Moses' hopes did not dim. He persisted in calling on her until one evening she told him firmly and clearly that he should not return. She did not want to see him again.

Moses threw caution to the wind. This would be the last time he could get a foot in the door so he asked an intriguing question: "Do you believe that marriages are made in Heaven?"

"Yes," replied Frumte hesitantly, reluctant in the insecurity of not knowing where he was headed with this. "I suppose so."

"So do I," agreed Moses. "You see, in Heaven, just before a boy is born, God shows him the girl he will someday marry. When God pointed out my future bride to me, God explained that she would be born with a hideous hunch back. That is when I asked God if he would please prevent the tragedy of a beautiful girl with a hunchback. I asked God to let the hunch back fall on me instead."

Frumte's eyes filled with tears. Years later she wrote, "I looked into the distance and I felt some long hidden memory stir in my heart. At that moment I realized the depth and quality of this deformed young man. I never regretted marrying him."

Shifting Gears

Maybe Moses Mendelssohn overplayed his hand in conjuring scenes of pre-natal heaven. Still, there is something quite insightful about his analysis of who we are in ourselves and what lies inside the persons we meet day to day. For one thing, there is something of divine beauty in every person knit together by God in each mother's womb. We did not emerge into this existence by our own volition or at the design of our own hand. And if our lives are a divine gift we ought to be careful about artificial criteria of worth we might use as plumb lines in measuring the bent of another soul.

Second, though physical realities, including beauty and social status, may initially mark our assessments of each other, they rarely tell the whole story of human meaning. "Poor eyes limit your sight," said Franklin Field. "Poor vision limits your deeds."

He knew us well. Who wants to kiss a hairlip? Who wants to hold hands with a stump destroyed by meat tenderizer mistakenly injected by a junkie (she was in our church telling her story recently)? Who wants to form "spoons" in bed with a hunchback? Perhaps only those whose vision is not encumbered with limited perspective and thus have eyes to see the true person. Some might say it is only those who love.

Stepping Through The Door Into Tomorrow

Third, there is something refreshing about stumbling into the Kingdom of God and finding relationships of meaning that are not prejudged and limited by the rules of others. By the rules of the day Frumte should not have married Felix. Similarly, Sir Walter Scott should not have remained with his disfigured wife. Likewise, Hosea should have divorced his wayward spouse. There are millions of other relationships that ought to have dissolved, at least on our terms. But what a serendipitous delight to find power in the passions of heaven!

"You have insulted the poor!" said James. Too bad! See what you missed? You missed the gifts God lavishly showered in unlikely corners. You missed a beauty beyond status. And you missed Jesus himself, because he was playing ball with the kids down that very alley.

25

(In)Security

"Is it not the rich who are exploiting you? Are they not the ones who are dragging you into court? Are they not the ones who are slandering the noble name of him to whom you belong?" (James 2:6)

When a young girl came home from Sunday School, her parents asked her about the lesson. "It was about a man who was traveling from Jerusalem to Jericho," she said. "He was beaten up by some bad men, and they threw his body into the ditch. Then two preachers came along, but when they saw that the man had already been robbed and they couldn't get anything more from him, they passed by on the other side!"

She along with many others seems to think that the church is always on the take, always asking for money. It's just another robber, merely pretending to be sanctified by the piety of religious language. Dennis the Menace, in one of the comic strips, also believes that the church is about money. As he drags his parents off to church on a Sunday morning, later than usual, he says, "I hope we get in our seats before they serve the money!" We all know that the "serve" is really the weekly "take."

"Who? Me?"

The mega-church campuses of today, with their multi-million dollar buildings ringed by fleets of expensive motor vehicles, would likely have surprised James. He didn't have a great view of a money/religion mix, nor could he seem to connect wealthy people with God.

Of course, we're quick to point out the sociological changes that have taken place since his days, and the fact that upper middle class folk, as well as rich people, have done a world of good in the church and kingdom with their money. We'd be quick to tell James that his comments were for the godless rich of his day, and that we use our financial resources in a different way. But as Shakespeare said through Hamlet, "The lady doth protest too much, methinks!" The Bride of Christ certainly finds her fiscal welfare changed since James' days and, perhaps more than she would care to admit, her spiritual outlook along with it. At the height of the Middle Ages theologian Thomas Aquinas paused with the pope as a new shipment of offerings and artistic masterpieces entered the Vatican. Reflecting on Peter's words to the paralytic beggar in Acts 5 the pope commented, "No longer do we have to say, 'Silver and gold have I none.'"

With a sadly satirical twist of wit Aquinas replied, "Neither can we any longer say, 'In the name of Christ, rise up and walk.'"

How Much Security Do You Need?

What makes money so important to us? At least in part it seems to be connected with our perceptions of security. Don Marquis rightly said, "There is nothing so habit-forming as money." Researchers claim that the major concern of most college and university students is getting the right education to land the right job in order to make the right amount of money. Money is perceived of as power and security—the more you have of it, the more you have of them.

A story of tandem bikers is telling. Riding their two-seater along a highway they encountered a steep hill. Panting and groaning, they finally achieved the summit.

"What a climb!" said one when they stopped for a rest break.

"Yeah!" said the other. "And if I hadn't kept the brake on, we would have slid right down again!"

That's often a picture of us, racing through life. We puff up the ladder of success, expanding our earnings while gripping the brake ever more tightly, scared of what might happen if we ever let go. Years ago I sat with a man at a coffee shop. I was new in town and he wanted to sell me some life insurance.

"How much security do you want?" he asked me. He had been a wheeler-dealer in Calgary during the oil boom, earning big money, living fast times. Then the boom went bust, his investments collapsed, and his wife left with another high roller. Now he was back in his hometown trying to start over.

"How much security can you offer?" I responded. His eyes lit up. His face got flushed. He was ready to move in for the deal. But then we started talking about the church. It soon became apparent that he had another agenda tucked behind his tycoon come-on. Did I really believe all this religion stuff? Could God really love him after all he'd done, after the mess he'd made of things? He'd been on the fast track: bright lights, big city. He wanted desperately to be loved, but one marriage was gone and another relationship was souring. Money bought him nothing. Was there something more?

Who Owns Whom?

I could see my own heart reflected in his flush and fears. We are all looking for security. We think we can find it in money, in wealth, in possessions. And maybe for a while it works.

But one day Jesus comes along, like he did that day in Jericho when he met Zachaeus. And when he tells us that he loves us, and when he tells us that his father is taking care of us, we can finally let our grabbing fists go, and ease the pain of our ulcers, and give away the possessions that have begun to possess us.

Ernest Hemingway used to give away some of his most valued possessions at the beginning of each new year. He said he did it to prove that he really owned them, and not the other way around. If he couldn't give them away, they owned him. They controlled his heart.

That brings us back to James' words. Why is he so hard on the rich? For the same reason Jesus was. Everybody can get into the Kingdom of God. It's just harder when you don't think you need it.

26

Building a Heaven in Hell's Despair

"If you really keep the royal law found in Scripture, 'Love your neighbor as yourself,' you are doing right. But if you show favoritism, you sin and are convicted by the law as lawbreakers." (James 2:8-9)

South of London, Ontario, Canada, the highways are lined with apple orchards. Every fall one farmer was chagrined when cars pulled to the side of the road and people jumped out to raid his trees. Most often, even if they saw him watching them they would hop back over the fence, get in the car again, and speed away before he could do anything.

One day when it happened again, however, the owner was ready. When a family returned to their car, arms bulging with apples, they found him leaning against the fender. Sheepishly they apologized and said, "We hope you don't mind that we took a few of your apples."

"No," said the farmer, "not at all. And I hope you don't mind that I took some of the air out of your tires."

Revenge

Revenge comes easily to us, doesn't it? Manolo Ramos of Barcelona, Spain, ran a little restaurant that proved nicely profitable until a former acquaintance opened a similar eating establishment just down the street. So Ramos gathered the neighborhood youngsters and asked if they wanted to make a little money. He gave them coins, passed out sticks of gum, and told them to chew it and spit it out on the sidewalk in front of his competitor's restaurant. After all, a man has to protect his business.

Of course, that thirst for vengeance coughs in another throat as well. Ramos eventually spent several months of penitent time in jail and lost a bunch of his profits in a fine equivalent to $1,500.00. So it goes in our world. What goes around comes around.

Point of Faith

C. S. Lewis said that it was precisely through his reflections on the consistency of human revenge that he became a Christian. He was amazed that peoples of all cultures similarly demanded to have their "rights" protected. A child fights to hang on to a toy in a nursery. A man attacks the one who scratched the paint on his new car. A woman feeds the gossip network to get back at someone who wronged her. It's the stuff of the office scramble. It's the vicious competition fostered in schools and colleges. It's the thing on which societies hang their hats and load their guns.

Before Lewis became a Christian all of this strength of moral indignation tormented his soul. How could there be a universal craving for justice without some Higher Power to plant it as a seed in the human spirit, or standing as a final arbiter behind all things moral? Even where I may not be entirely honest or have full integrity, there is an urgent sense of "rights" at work within me. When Lewis relentlessly pursued the trail of moral responsibility it led him back to God.

On Beyond Justice

It was then, according to Lewis, that a new order of values took over. Even though thirst for justice in some form is universal, the logic of justice ultimately breaks down. For one thing, none of us is ever as righteous in our own lives as the moral behavior we expect from others. In other words, we will always attempt to lay a heavier burden on those around us than we are willing to submit to ourselves. Even where we excuse society generally as being immoral we will want others to treat us with great justice and more. This double standard fosters a plague of moral decay since we cannot retain human dignity when we will destroy each other on the logic of justice untempered by mercy.

That brought Lewis a second stage in his quest for a new order of things. He read about Jesus. Jesus, he realized, fully met the demands of God's justice but did so in such a way that, as the Psalmist put it, in God "love and faithfulness meet together; righteousness and peace kiss each other!" (Psalm 85:10).

The logic of justice serves well to prove the reality of God's presence in this world, as Paul talked about it in Romans 2. Yet justice alone leaves us fainting for a quality of life that transcends the fear of both human and divine vengeance that justice brings. Only when we meet Jesus do we find something greater than mere justice. And only then can we go beyond the favoritism that James rues in order to love with the grace of mercy.

"I find myself wishing him well."

Lew Smedes explores this in terms we all understand as he tells of his friend Myra Broger. Myra is a beautiful woman, he says, an actress. Some years ago she was nearly killed by a hit-and-run driver. Now she is crippled.

At the time of the accident Myra was married to another actor. He stayed around long enough to be certain that Myra didn't die from the accident. Then he left her. He divorced her because he couldn't be encumbered by her crippled weight. Now he is off with other women who aren't crippled.

Myra hated him for it, according to Smedes. She resented him for what he did to her. She despised him for the vows he broke, and detested him for the meanness that left her alone just when she needed him most.

After several years Lew Smedes asked her if she had ever been able to forgive her ex-husband. She thought about it for a while, finally nodding her head with slow deliberation. Yes, she said, she believed she had begun to forgive him.

Smedes was curious. How did she come to that conclusion? How could she tell if she had forgiven him?

Myra Broger's answer was simple. "I find myself wishing him well," she said.

Smedes was unsure how to interpret that, so he asked a follow-up question. "Myra," he said, "suppose you learned today that he had married a sexy young starlet... Could you pray that he would be happy with her?"

Smedes says he expected her to bristle at the thought, but she didn't. She responded almost casually, he says. "Yes, I could and I would," she said. "Steve needs love very much, and I want him to have it."

That is not a blazing declaration of absolution for his crimes, but it is a crack in hell's armor. As William Blake put it in one of his poems:

> **Love seeketh not itself to please,**
>
> **Nor for itself hath any care,**
>
> **But for another gives its ease,**
>
> **And builds a Heaven in Hell's despair.**

27

On Beyond Perfection

"For whoever keeps the whole law and yet stumbles at just one point is guilty of breaking all of it. For he who said, "Do not commit adultery," also said, "Do not murder." If you do not commit adultery but do commit murder, you have become a lawbreaker." (James 2:10-11)

Dr. Seuss had a wonderful way of making the ordinary extraordinary. In is book *On Beyond Zebra* he noted that most people quit far too soon when they learn the alphabet. Starting out at "A is for Apple," they go all the way through the twenty-six letters to "Z is for Zebra" and then think they are finished.

Not so Dr. Seuss! Twenty-six letters might be good enough for others, but Dr. Seuss has only just begun. In his book, one of his delightful little people takes readers on a tour of the world that's *"On Beyond Zebra,"* where the colors are more brilliant, the shapes eccentric, and the creatures marvelously different from those in our drab A-to-Z existence.

Worried to Death

It seems that James lives in a similar world, one that is "on beyond perfection." It is a world where morality seems far to exceed not merely breaking the law. One must almost live *above* the law, it would seem, not just in some superiority-complex way but also with eyes that are not glued to the rulebook and a heart that has gotten beyond even fussing about it.

Sometimes religious people can be too concerned about correct ethical behavior, making it an end in itself. A cartoon in the *New Yorker* showed a man newly dead standing at the gate of heaven. He is in an intense conversation with the apostle Peter. Nervous beads of perspiration dot his forehead, and he is wringing his hands in anxiety as he tries to give a good account of his life.

Peter shakes his head. "No, no, no!" he says. "That's not a sin either! My goodness! You must have worried yourself to death!"

A morality of perfection focuses only on keeping the law. In itself that is, of course, quite a worrisome task. But the morality of Christ with which James concerns himself is one that focuses on the relationship that originally produced the "law" for the people of God.

Loved to Life

Professor Ed Dowey, retired from Princeton Seminary, used to talk about that. He said, "Suppose I'm walking down the street today, just minding my business, and I meet someone I don't even know. Suppose, that for some reason, out of the clear blue, she smiles at me. Now my heart is suddenly warmed. And what happens, but a smile pops out of my heart, and onto my lips too! That's grace.

"But suppose that tomorrow I'm out there walking again and I see her coming toward me. Do you know what happens? Before she even catches sight of my face today, I start wearing a smile. You know why? Because in my heart I'm hoping I can get her to smile at me again!"

Says Dowey, "That's legalism!" Grace happens; legalism tries to make it work.

And so it is in our morality of behavior. Perfection keeps us toeing the line, while a relationship with Jesus Christ, and with others through him, gives us grace to keep our eyes on people, not the rulebook.

Marked by Grace

Thomas Long told about the examination of ministerial candidates in a North Carolina Presbytery. One elderly minister always kept quiet through the bulk of the ordeals, according to Long, and then invariably asked the same final set of questions just at the close of each examination.

"Look out that window," he would order the candidates. "Tell me when you see someone walking out there." So they did. When someone walked by he would say, "Now, describe that person to me *theologically*."

Each person's answer would be a bit different from the others, of course. Yet they consistently could be reduced to just two basic ideas. One group of ministers-to-be would say something like: "Well, there goes a sinner who is on his way to hell unless he repents!"

The other group responded something like this: "There goes a person who is a child of God. God loves that person so very much, and the best thing that can happen to him is to find out how good it is to love God in return!"

Funny thing, said the old minister, both responses are probably right. Still, those who respond in the latter way always make better pastors.

Why? Because they have learned to live life on beyond perfection. For when the roll is called up yonder, the grades on the report cards that make it won't be "A" for excellent, or "B" for good, or even "C" for nice try. The only grade that will make it will be "G".

For Grace.

28

The Wit to Win

"Speak and act as those who are going to be judged by the law that gives freedom, because judgment without mercy will be shown to anyone who has not been merciful. Mercy triumphs over judgment!"

(James 2:12-13)

In 1967 a psychologist named Kinch reported a rather bizarre experiment conducted by university psychology graduate students. These males were part of what they considered to be the "in" crowd on campus. They moved in the right circles, dressed the right way and went to the right places for nightlife parties.

But they all knew a particular young woman who wasn't in that circle. She was an "outsider," a "nobody," a person who didn't count, at least to them and their kind.

Knowing the effects of behavior modification, they planned together to see how she would change if they treated her, for a time, as if she were part of their "in" crowd. They made an agreement that whenever they saw her they would compliment her and show an interest in her. Furthermore, they would take turns asking her out on dates.

Turning Tables

The experiment took a strange turn. Under other circumstances they did not like her. They would not have talked *to* her prior to this, but only *about* her, and in condescending and cynical ways. Yet as the challenge progressed each of the men gradually found the young woman more likable, less foreign, less alien. The first fellow's date with her went okay, even though he had to keep telling himself she was more beautiful and better company than he truly felt.

But by the time the third fellow asked her out, she had actually become part of their circle of friends. They thought it was kind of fun being with her. She wasn't so bad after all!

And the fifth fellow never did get to date her, because the fourth fellow in line asked her to be his wife! What started as a rather cruel experiment ended up as an amazing testimony to the truth of James' words. The judgments made by the "in" group of men proved paltry in the face of mercy, even if it began as a psychological exercise.

Edwin Markham put it well when he wrote:

He drew a circle that shut me out ---

Heretic! Rebel! A thing to flout!

But love and I had the wit to win:

We drew a circle that took him in!

Love's Labors Gained

We are taught fair play as children, seeking a place to hang onto our "rights." That is a good thing. But the law made for children, as both Paul and James declare in the New Testament, must eventually give way to relationships of mercy that reflect the spiritual maturity of our true Father.

Sometimes there are children who can show this in remarkable ways as Dale Galloway related in his book *Dream a New Dream* (Tyndale, 1975). A friend's son was very shy, he said. Chad was usually by himself, and others took no effort to include him in their circles of friends. Every afternoon Chad's mother would see the children would pile off the school bus in groups, laughing, playing, and joking around with each other. Chad, however, would always be the last down the steps, always alone. No one ever paid much attention to him.

One day in late January Chad came home and said, "You know what, Mom? Valentine's Day is coming and I want to make a valentine for everyone in my class!"

Chad's mother told Dale how terrible she felt. "Oh no!" she thought. "Chad is setting himself up for a fall now. He's going to make valentines for everyone else, but nobody will think of him. He'll come home all disappointed, and just pull back further into his shell."

But Chad insisted, so they got paper and crayons and glue. Chad made thirty-one valentine cards. It took him three weeks.

The day he took them to school his mother cried a lot. When he came off the bus alone as usual, bearing no valentine cards from others in his hands, she was ready for the worst.

Amazingly Chad's face was glowing. He marched through the door triumphant. "I didn't forget anybody!" he said. "I gave them all one of my hearts!"

That day Chad gained something more than just friends. He gained a sense of himself. He won a sense of dignity and worth. "I gave them all one of my hearts!" he said.

Coming Home

That's where James wants to bring us. Circles of hatred erased by circles of love. Circles of judgment blurred by widening circles of mercy. Circles of Death that give way to circles of Life. The gospel says that when we had drawn God out of our circles, his love drew us in. Perhaps Markham's poem could be translated into the conversation of heaven as the Father and the Son reflect about me:

> **He drew a circle that shut us out ---**
>
> **Heretic! Rebel! A thing to flout!**
>
> **But our love alone had the wit to win:**

96

We drew a circle that took him in!

That was the day Mercy triumphed over Justice!

29

Responsible Living

"What good is it, my brothers, if a man claims to have faith but has no deeds? Can such faith save him? Suppose a brother or sister is without clothes and daily food. If one of you says to him, "Go, I wish you well; keep warm and well fed," but does nothing about his physical needs, what good is it? In the same way, faith by itself, if it is not accompanied by action, is dead." (James 2:14-16)

Lee Sharpe remembers a childhood incident that made a permanent impact on his life. It was the spring of the year and his father wanted to get the garden ready for planting. When he took his hoe and rake from the shed both needed repair. He dropped them off at Trussel's blacksmith shop saying, "Whenever you can get around to it, I'd appreciate it if you could fix these. I know it's not much, and I hate to bother you with it."

Stretching One's Soul

Mr. Trussel said it was no problem; he'd look after it. Several days later he called to say that the tools were fixed and ready. Mr. Sharpe could pick them up anytime.

Lee went with his father that afternoon to get them. Mr. Trussel had done a fine job. But when Lee's Dad asked, "How much do I owe you?" Mr. Trussel shrugged his shoulders and replied, "Don't worry about it. My pleasure."

That didn't sit right with Mr. Sharpe. He was a fair man and wanted to pay a fair price for a fair hour of work. He took out his wallet and tried to shove some money into Mr. Trussel's hands. The blacksmith, however, adamantly refused. He held up his hands and said, "Sid, can't you let a man do something now and then, just to stretch his soul?"

Young Lee carried that incident with him for the rest of his life. It was, for him, a vision of integrity: Mr. Trussel spoke and lived the faith he believed.

Beyond "Easy" Street

Henry Ward Beecher spoke of the morality of Christian faith like this: "Religion means work. Religion means work in a dirty world. Religion means peril... Religion means transformation. The world is to be cleaned by somebody; and you are not called of God if you are ashamed to scour and scrub."

He was only echoing the truth of James' teaching. Sometimes we make too little of our faith. We let it become too tiny, too private, too pious. But the Christianity that James writes about is a deep Christianity. James calls himself a "slave" of Jesus Christ (1:1). And when he thinks about what Jesus went through, there are a lot of words that could be used---tremendous! incredible! overwhelming! awesome! But when you look at the cross of Jesus one word that can never be used is "easy"! To call it that would be a sacrilege!

The same is true for an "easy" Christianity that buttons itself up in the coziness of warm feelings and private thoughts, without clothing others and acting on principles of moral responsibility. James would call such an attitude sin.

A Faith That Matters

Even Charles Darwin was impressed by Christian faith that breathed through responsible Christian living. He had disowned the Christianity of his childhood, and was sailing for five years around South America in search of confirmation to his theories of natural selection and evolutionary development. When he stopped for a while at Tierra del Fuego he found a community that defied his prescriptions for normal human development. Under the teaching and ministry of a man named Thomas Bridges the whole society was being transformed into something better than it used to be.

The power in Thomas Bridges' leadership came from his own story. He was abandoned as a baby on the banks of the Thames in London, England. Passers-by heard his feeble cries and rescued him barely alive. It happened on St. *Thomas'* Day near several *bridges* over the river, so they called him Thomas Bridges. The family that raised him as their own gave him confidence in the love of Jesus. Though abandoned by his mother, he learned the power of faith that lives through deeds of those who care.

That is why he became a missionary of Jesus Christ, and the reason his words, coupled with actions, rang with power. Even Charles Darwin, as he was becoming an atheist, supported Thomas Bridges financially for the rest of his life. Here was faith that made a difference, and that was something the world needed more than another scientific theory.

30

The Shape of Faith

"In the same way, faith by itself, if it is not accompanied by action, is dead. But someone will say, 'You have faith; I have deeds.' Show me your faith without deeds, and I will show you my faith by what I do."

(James 2:17-18)

A young girl stood sobbing near a small church. It was the only church in her very poor neighborhood of Philadelphia. The auditorium was full, and some were being turned away for lack of room. There were too many children crowding the building, so this girl couldn't attend Sunday School.

A man stopped by her, kneeling to find what was wrong. He was the pastor of the congregation. Upon hearing her story he decided that if she wanted to go to Sunday School so desperately he would create a place for her, no matter what it took. So the girl became a regular member of a Sunday School class at that church.

Pauper's Pennies

Two years later she died in a poverty-stricken high-rise tenement apartment. Her parents asked the pastor to help them arrange for a funeral. They gave the pastor a tiny, dirty purse. Their young daughter had salvaged it in from garbage can and kept it under her pillow. Inside were fifty-seven pennies

101

and a crumpled note in childish handwriting: "This is to help build the little church bigger so more children can go to Sunday School."

The next Sunday that pastor took the cracked red pocketbook with him to the congregation. He told the story of the young girl's sense of self, and the generosity of her deep devotion.

The story didn't end there. It was reported by someone in the Philadelphia newspaper. A realtor came to the board of deacons and offered a large parcel of prime land worth many thousands of dollars. The church couldn't afford to buy it, but the realtor said he only wanted a down payment of fifty-seven cents.

Others were spurred on to take a second look at their sense of self and their acts of devotion to God and to the Church. Soon costly gifts began to pour in.

Sacred Stones

Today, if you go to Philadelphia, you can find Temple Baptist Church. It seats 3300 people at one time and has many, many rooms for Sunday School classes. On the same parcel of ground is Temple University, which graduates hundreds of students every year, equipped, in some way, for service in the Kingdom of God. Next to them stand Good Samaritan Hospital. You can imagine what happens there.

How did these ministries develop? Not because anybody gave money to the church. Rather, because a young girl saved fifty-seven pennies to give to God as a costly sacrifice of devotion. And because a realtor sacrificed his livelihood for a gift in celebration of Christ's love. And because a poor community checked its identity, and gave great gifts of sacrifice to make the name of God greater in the city of Philadelphia.

31

Faith Comes in Two Layers

"You believe that there is one God. Good! Even the demons believe that---and shudder." (James 2:19)

John Calvin said that there were two aspects to faith: *assentia* and *fiducia*. The first we often translate as "assent." It is in this dimension of faith that we acknowledge that something exists. *Assentia* is knowing something factually, or knowing about someone only from a distance.

Calvin's second aspect of faith might well be termed "trust." It is a heart engagement, involving us personally in an emotional attachment with whatever we might have previously acknowledged only intellectually.

Sitting on our faith

Take a chair, for instance. *Assentia* is our willingness to say that it could hold the person daring to sit on it. *Fiducia*, on the other hand, is the act of sitting on that chair ourselves, trusting its sturdiness to hold our bulk. Both are elements of faith. Both are important. But until the latter is added to the former, faith remains inert, distant, intellectual, impersonal. That is why, according to James, the demons, who have no intention of trusting God (*fiducia*) do still have a kind of faith in God (*assentia*).

James is offering a strong incentive for us to get beyond talking about God and getting on with the business of engaging God as an active partner in our lives. Faith talk means little if we carry on conversations one might just as easily hear in hell.

Dr. E. Stanley Jones told of an incident from his missionary days that illustrates James' point. A young girl got tired of things at home, said Jones. She longed for the freedom of the streets, and the excitement of the nightlife. She ran away to a large city. It wasn't long before she fell under the spell of a pimp and was degraded into a prostitute.

Restless and Protective

The girl's mother was beside herself with anxiety. It was true that things hadn't been going right between them, but a mother's love is restless and protective, and she had to find her daughter again. She remembered the child who sat on her lap, and the daughter who whispered in her ear, and needed somehow to renew their bond of trust.

Yet how should she begin the search? All she had heard were rumors about daughter, third-hand reports that she was now wasting her body in the red-light district. The mother went to the city and simply began to walk, hoping to stumble across someone who might know her daughter. Up one street and down the next she trudged, talking to anyone who would listen, hoping for a clue to follow.

But to no avail. Her daughter didn't want to be found: shame; rebellion, spite... Who can say what reasons mingle in our deceptive minds?

A Picture is worth a thousand Words

Eventually the quest tired even the mother. But before she returned home, she did one more thing. She carried a photograph that had been taken several years before, a picture of the two of them, mother and daughter, at a happier moment in both their lives. She got the photograph enlarged and made dozens of copies. Then she scattered those pictures around the area, hoping that one would catch her daughter's eye.

On each photo she penned these five words: **Come home! I love you!**

And one day the girl did see. She began to remember what love was all about. A holy restless gripped her soul, battering her resentment until she had to call her mother. The next day she was home.

Never once did the daughter stop *assenting* to the fact that she had a mother. But it wasn't until her mother's love called out the *trust* of her heart that she believed in all that "home" and "mother" and "love" could mean to her personally.

If James were to take a picture of your faith today, how much depth would it show?

32

Abraham

"You foolish man, do you want evidence that faith without deeds is useless? Was not our ancestor Abraham considered righteous for what he did when he offered his son Isaac on the altar?" (James 2:20-21)

You remember the story... Abraham was a great old man, probably 125 or so! God had come to him in the past in strange and wonderful ways. When he wore a younger man's clothes, the VOICE had called him on a journey with no fixed destination. But the beckoning was always one of blessing: "I'll give you land beyond measure! I'll make sure you have a child, old as you are! Your descendants will populate these hills and valleys like rain!"

Well, the land sort of took him in. Moreover, after some fits and starts he and Sarai did get a child. And even though his pension plan was still not entirely clear, life in these later years was peaceful and prosperous. After all, there was Isaac. His boy's name meant "Laughter!" and that's certainly what he brought Abraham these days. Life had turned out okay.

A Darker Chapter

Now the VOICE came to him again. But was it really the same VOICE? "Sacrifice your son Isaac on the altar to me!" it said. What kind of God was this? Or was it perhaps a demon's mocking mimic?

"Kill your boy! Choke out the Laughter!" God forbid! Please, God, let it not be so!

There would be no sleep this night. Abraham's mind whirls while his old bones crawl in pain. *Get the servants... Get the transportation... Get provisions... Get wood... Get the son...*

Three days travel they go, with every step harder than the last. Isaac chatters his usual banter, laughter echoing in Abraham's cold heart. Reluctantly Abraham spies the high place finally. The mountain of doom. The plateau of death.

Strangely gruff, Abraham orders the servants to stay. "The boy and I will go it alone from here." Two on a murderous mission. Only one will return. The father-son hike soured even more when Isaac's laughter lilted a deadly chilly question: "Where's the lamb, father?"

Mockery

What could Abraham say? Does he tell Isaac the truth: "Son, the God who said he loved me enough to give you to your mother and I now says he wants you back, and I've got to do the dirty work!"? How do you lie with a straight face when heaven is ripped apart by hell? Is it a spiteful retort, spat out in unholy jest, that finally clears his throat: "My son, God will provide..."?

So here they are, clearing and building and preparing. And now the end creeps with horror into Isaac's eyes. His father binds him. His father thrusts him on the wood. His father stands over him with a glinting knife. And the Laughter dies...

But not yet. In a miraculous moment, time stops and grace points to another sacrifice. The son is free, and faith is affirmed. And he calls the place **Moriah**.

Moriah is one of those delightfully ambiguous names that can mean several things at once. It probably has to do with seeing at this point, or knowing. Where God sees, he will be seen. Something like that.

A Strange Vision

But what is it that God sees on a mountain called Moriah? For one thing, he sees a man. A weak man. A stumbler on the earth. A business man who got ahead in life. A husband who cheated on his wife. A father who knew the joy of bringing new life into being.

Even more than that God sees a man who was willing to put it all on the line. Here was someone who counted his relationship with the God of the VOICE to be the one thing that mattered, the one thing that put everything else together, the one thing that could raise even heaven out of this stench of hell.

Probably the most important thing about the moment of seeing is not only that God sees Abraham there on Mount Moriah. In some mysterious way God is also seen by Abraham.

A geography lesson tells the rest of the story. On this same barren spot of ground, centuries later, David would urge Solomon to build the Temple of God. It would stand as a doorway between earth and eternity. And then, in the mysterious design of the ages, one day another Father would walk these slopes with another Son. That Son, too, would raise his voice to his Father, and the Father, for a time would be silent. The wood of the offering would be prepared, and the Son would be lifted as a sacrifice. On what the world would later call "Good Friday" this other Father would shed tears of pain as his Child died, this time with no escape.

Somehow history would repeat itself and more with a vengeance. Yet this Lamb would also be chosen by God for the altar. And Laughter would be silenced for three days while all the world looked on in wonder.

The Language of Faith

Abraham found his faith that day on Mount Moriah, but it cost God his Son on the same spot. The mystery of life is found now not in a faith that pretends Laughter, but in a promise that God knows Pain. Because he has walked a mile in Abraham's shoes and ours, God will never leave us. He will never forsake us.

The poet put it powerfully:

> **Often you wondered why tears came into your eyes**
>
> **And burdens seem to be much more than you can stand.**
>
> **But God is standing near; he sees your falling tears.**
>
> **Tears are a language God understands!**
>
>> **God sees the tears of a broken-hearted soul.**
>>
>> **He sees your tears, and hears them when they fall.**
>>
>> **God weeps along with man, and takes him by the hand.**
>>
>> **Tears are a language God understands!**

33

When Faith Grows Up

"You see that his faith and his actions were working together, and his faith was made complete by what he did" (James 2:22)

Fred Craddock and his wife were on vacation in the Great Smoky Mountains of eastern Tennessee when they stumbled onto an out-of-the-way restaurant called the Black Bear Inn. It proved to be a good place to eat, besides offering the possibility of actually seeing one of those black bears. An entire wall was glass, opening out onto a wild and rugged valley.

As they sat at supper, quietly communing with nature and each other, their solitude was broken by a tall man with a shock of white hair who ambled over. They could see he was well along in years, probably past the fourscore allotted by the Psalmist.

Tale of Woe

He was hard of hearing as well, since he rudely interrupted their quiet reverie with noisy and nosy questions at least 20 decibels too loud. When he found that Fred taught at a seminary he suddenly had a story to tell about preachers. Without an invitation he pulled up a chair and invaded their space.

Nodding out the great glass window, he said, "I was born back here in these mountains."

But the story was not to be a pretty one. "My mother was not married," he went on, "and the reproach that fell upon her, fell upon me. The children at school had a name for me, and it hurt. It hurt very much."

In fact, he said, "During recess I would go hide in the weeds until the bell rang. At noon hour I took my lunch and went behind a tree to avoid them. And when I went to town with my mamma, all the grownups would stop and stare at us. They'd look at my mamma, and then they'd look at me, and I could see they were trying to guess who my Daddy might have been. Painful years, those."

Tidings of Grace

But something big was about to happen. "I guess it was about the seventh or eight grade," he continued, "when a preacher came to town. He frightened me when he preached, and he attracted me, all at the same time. He was a big man. Thundered when he preached. But he caught me. Every time he preached he caught me with his words.

"I didn't want the people to catch me, though. So I never went to church on time. Waited around outside till they sang the hymn before the sermon. Then I'd sneak in just as he was getting warmed up. When he was finished I'd rush right out. Didn't want to hear the people say, 'What's a boy like you doin' in church?'

"But one morning I got caught. A bunch of women lined up in the aisle, and I couldn't get out. And I got all nervous and cold and sweaty. And I knew somebody was going to see me and say, 'Whatcha doin' here, boy? What's a boy like you doin' in church?'

"And sure enough, suddenly a hand clamped down on my shoulder. Out of the corner of my eye I could see the preacher's face.

"'Whoa, boy!' he says to me. And he turns me around, and he looks me in the face. And he studies me for a while. And I can just see he's trying to find the family resemblance. And finally he says, 'Well, boy...! I can see it now...! I can see you're a child of... You're a child of... Wait now...'

111

"And he stared me right in the face. 'Yep!' he says. 'I can see it now! You're a child of... God! There's a striking resemblance!'

"Then that preacher man swatted me on the bottom, and he said, 'Go on, boy! Go claim your family inheritance!'"

Testimonies of Life

The Craddock's were quite taken by the story the old man had to tell. Fred thought there was something familiar about it, so he asked the elderly gent, "Sir, what's your name?"

The man replied, proudly, "Ben Hooper!"

It was then that Fred Craddock remembered his Daddy telling him the story of the time the people of Tennessee twice elected an illegitimate bastard boy as governor, and how Ben Hooper had done the state proud.

Ben Hooper had faith. He gained faith when a preacher told him he was child of God. He proved his faith when he carved a future of grace out of a mixed inheritance. Or, as James puts it, "...his faith was made complete by what he did."

34

Credit

"And the scripture was fulfilled that says, 'Abraham believed God, and it was credited to him as righteousness...'" (James 2:23)

A gracious woman in the latter half of her life was once giving advice to a marriage preparation class that I organized. When it comes to making purchases, she told the young women of the group, "Don't ever buy anything on credit. Always pay for everything with cash."

Incredulous laughter rippled around the room. Can you imagine a modern wallet with no credit cards in it?

Honest Poverty, Dishonest Wealth

Financial credit is a strange thing. You can't get it if you don't have it. And when you try to have it, it doesn't belong to you anyway. When we moved to Michigan from Canada, our credit rating didn't follow us. Before we built our home, no credit card company would issue us one in spite of the fact that we had thousands of dollars in the bank. Once we moved into our new home, heavily mortgaged, the offers came nearly every day: "You have been pre-approved for $5000.00 credit!" How could that be?

When the German poet Detlez von Liliencron was in a tight financial bind one of his creditors stopped him on the street and demanded payment. "Sorry," he said, "but I have no money. Please be patient."

The man was indignant. Stammering irately, he replied, "But that's what you said four weeks ago!"

"Well," said Liliencron triumphantly, "haven't I kept my word?"

I don't suppose that kind of credit sat well with his creditor.

Songs of Self

Credit is a slippery thing. You may want it, but if you mention that, you won't likely get it. In fact, you might even get blacklisted instead. Gilbert and Sullivan have their Captain of the *H. M. S. Pinafore* proclaiming his eminent worth in their operetta of that name. Behind him a chorus declaims and defames: "He is an Englishman! For he himself has said it, And it's greatly to his credit, That he is an Englishman!" All the while, of course, the audience is laughing at his buffoonery.

Sometimes we look for credit by association. In the last years of his life, composer Louis Antoine Jullien dreamed of writing one final work. He said he would like to set the words of the Lord's Prayer to music. Wouldn't it look wonderful, he asked his colleagues, to have a title page that read: *THE LORD'S PRAYER. Words by Jesus Christ. Music by Jullien.*?

The best credit, of course, is neither earned nor grasped. One of my favorite stories about Abraham Lincoln comes from his Illinois days as a young lawyer. An angry man stormed into his office demanding that he bring suit against an impoverished debtor who owed him $2.50. "Make him pay!"

Well, Lincoln didn't want anything of the sort to happen. The debtor couldn't pay the $2.50, the creditor didn't need the $2.50, and society shouldn't be run by either such greed or such insensitivity. So Lincoln declined the case.

When Grace Plays the Game

Unfortunately the man kept pressing, and since Lincoln was the only lawyer available, he was forced to serve the suit. First, though, he charged the man $10 for legal fees. Then he brought the defendant in, gave him $5.00 for his time, and asked if the charges were accurate. He readily agreed, and out of his newly gotten $5 paid the $2.50 he owed. Everyone was satisfied, including the irate plaintiff, who never realized that he spent $10 to collect $2.50!

Now turn that story around and think of it from this angle: A man with no credit is burdened by a debt he could never repay. Along comes an Advocate he can't hire to resolve a matter he can't win. Suddenly, in a transaction he could never accomplish, the debt is gone, the creditor has disappeared, and he has money in his pocket! All he had to do was agree to the terms.

So it is with faith, says James. Don't try to figure it out. And certainly don't claim credit for it. But when it's there, you'll know it.

And so will others!

35

Friend

When Pepper Rodgers was struggling through a terrible season as football coach at UCLA, everything in his life seemed to be going wrong. No one would speak with him. Even his home life was on edge and uncertain. "My dog was my only friend," he said. In fact, he mentioned that to his wife one day, telling her that a man really needs *two* friends. He was hoping to get a little sympathy from her. Instead she went out and bought him another dog!

Going Home to Ourselves

The Chinese have a saying: "When men are friendly even water is sweet!" And so it is. The character of the world is changed when friends surround us. Even our own selves warm up to greater things. As another old proverb puts it: "The best mirror is an old friend." When poet John Dryden penned an elegy in honor of his late friend Eleonora, his words showed how true that is:

> **The Souls of Friends like Kings in Progress are;**
>
> **Still in their own, though from the Palace far:**
>
> **Thus her Friend's Heart her Country Dwelling was,**

116

> **A sweet Retirement to a coarser place:**
>
> **Where Pomp and Ceremonies enter'd not;**
>
> **Where Greatness was shut out, and Bus'ness well forgot.**

Dryden's idea of a friend's heart serving as a "Country Dwelling" was powerfully revealed in a story Scott Camp told of a university student who was working on a doctorate investigating the social culture of the Navajo people. For a full year the young man lived with a Navajo family, participating in all the regimen and rituals of their lives.

Since Navajo households are often intergenerational, the grandmother, a wizened old woman, was matriarch of the home. She moved slowly and quietly among them, ever-present even without speaking. Though she knew little English, she soon became fast friends with the doctoral student. Somehow they shared a communication that needed few words. When the time finally came for him to leave, she uttered a single sentence that gathered into it the essence of what it means to be soul mates. She said: "I like me best when I'm with you!"

Echoing God's Heart

Queen Victoria of England said something similar when she reflected on two great men who had served the country for terms as Prime Minister. Of William Gladstone she opined, "When I am with him, I feel I am with one of the most important leaders in the world." On the other hand, she confessed that when she was with Disraeli, he made her feel "as if I am one of the most important leaders of the world."

A good friend brings out the best in us. Certainly God brought out the best in Abraham. That's understandable. But notice carefully the way James puts it. He doesn't say that God was Abraham's best friend, even though that was certainly the case. Instead, he tells us that Abraham was called a friend of God! There's something in our relationship with God that brings out the best in him too!

We call it grace, no matter which way it flows between friends. The *Pioneer Girls Leader's Handbook* says it this way: "A friend hears the song in my heart and sings it to me when my memory

117

fails." Maybe that's why God delights in our music. He'll never forget who he is so long as we keep singing *Amazing Grace.*

36

Actions Speak Louder than Words

"You see that a person is justified by what he does and not by faith alone." (James 2:24)

Arthur Clutton-Brock, who was for many years art critic for the London *Times*, wrote about his Christian faith in a book called *What Is the Kingdom of Heaven?* He tells a powerful story of his childhood.

He was out for a walk with his sitter, traipsing along a country lane. At a house just before them three children were romping through the yard, playing games and laughing delightedly. They had climbed a small sycamore tree, gathering leaves and tossing them into the air. The tender branches from the top of the tree, covered at the time with blazing bronzed leaves, they broke off and carried them in a bundle like a bouquet of flowers.

Haunted

When Arthur and his sitter passed by, the children ran out into the lane and danced about them. Then they presented the bouquet of branches to Arthur in a ceremony of great pomp. It was a magical moment of grace and beauty.

But for some reason, said Arthur, whether from fear or from pride, he refused the gift offered. He ran after his sitter and when they were shortly down the path he turned round to look at the three. He saw them standing in the middle of the road, faces suddenly dragging on the ground. The laughter was gone, and all the pretty flowers they had made were spilled around them in the dust.

Looking back on that moment Clutton-Brock said, "I felt, in that moment, that I had turned my back on the kingdom of God. Something had been offered to me in love, and I hadn't taken it!"

He also said that the sight of those three disappointed faces has haunted him all his life.

Hunted

The haunting of our lives is the gap between what we know to be truly significant and our own actions that betray days lived by secondary values and systems. A psychiatry textbook once carried this story of dissonance. A young lad with a rather evil temperament had met with every act of discipline his parents and school could mete. Still he rebelled and worked his cruel schemes.

But one summer's day, playing with the little dog that he had recently come to enjoy, he tried to teach the puppy a new trick. The afternoon was hot, the dog tired, and the boy impatient. When it failed to understand his commands, the lad lashed out with his foot, kicking it in the mouth till it bleed. Puzzled and bewildered, the dog crawled back to him, big brown eyes questioning in love. One front leg was broken. Still it humped its way to the boy's leg, and reached up a shaking paw. With a bleeding nose it sniffed at his arm and whimpered as it tried to lick his hand.

Home

The boy broke. He jumped to his feet and ran to the house blinded by tears. Sobbing in fits he threw himself into his mother's arms, repeating over and over, "I have done an awful thing!" Like the Prodigal Son of Jesus story in Luke 15, he was haunted back to his father.

So it is with faith. The words we speak in testimony mean little until our feet carry us home. That is why James is so insistent on reading our faith by what we do. What we believe is written in a story penned anew each day. The test of our relationship with God is not the bent of our theology but the grace with which we receive flowers of the Kingdom and the attitude we bear toward even the little puppies

God had made to romp in it.

37

Rahab

"In the same way, was not even Rahab the prostitute considered righteous for what she did when she gave lodging to the spies and sent them off in a different direction?" (James 2:25)

Adolph Hitler lived under the shadow of fear that someone might discover Jewish ancestry in his family line. His rage against the Jewish people can be explained, in part, on his own caustic humiliation at carrying "bad blood."

Modern psychology has taken some of the sting out of strange skeletons in the family closet. In fact, there are times we rattle the bones of scoundrels and imbibe the blood of exotic ancestors with relish. Maybe it's a way to excuse our darker deeds and passionate excesses.

Scandal!

But a prostitute in the family was no cause for cheer in ancient Israel. That's why the note including Rahab in Jesus' maternity in Matthew 1:5 is so striking. Rahab, we are told, married Salmon, and Boaz was their child—Boaz who married that foreigner Ruth, and got the family line of King David started.

Salmon must have been either a renegade Israelite or a man of larger-than-life proportions to take Rahab as his wife. There were at least three good reasons why he should not have married a prostitute, all of them religious.

First, children born to a prostitute could not claim paternity in the clan. Since a prostitute could not be trusted to keep her sperm selection pure, no one could legally press any man to father her children after birth or pass along the family farm to them. Although Paul speaks kindly of adoption in the New Testament and turns it into a theological construct of our relationship with God, the nation of Israel had virtually no guidelines or laws about it. A man was expected to know the children he fathered and he was supposed to take care of them. Orphans became the responsibility of the extended family. The children of prostitutes, however, did not rate a place in the community at all. So, even though men of Israel made use of prostitutes when traveling among other tribes and races, prostitution in Israel itself was virtually unknown. More than that, prostitutes didn't marry up-standing men.

Sinful!

Second, the holiness codes of Leviticus preserved Israel as the bride of Yahweh, married to him and reserved virginally pure to him. For that reason the worship of other gods was termed "prostitution" again and again. Since there was a relationship of sexual purity involved in Israel's relationship with God, all sexual deviation and perversion were clearly cast outside the camp as grotesquely sinful. Once again, prostitutes were not to marry into the tribes.

Third, much of prostitution in the ancient near east was connected with religious cultic rites. Prostitutes were often the harem of the gods, and when others spent time with them it was a way of rubbing up against the fertility of spiritual powers. If a man could get a prostitute pregnant it showed that he were blessed by the gods and vitally connected to them.

So why did the spies sent by Joshua to scout the defenses of Jericho end up hiding from the city police in the house of Rahab, a prostitute? Probably because their coming and going wouldn't raise too many eyebrows. After all, she had men sneaking in and out all the time. Besides, who would know more about the politics and defenses of Jericho than the one who has the bedroom ear of kings and city council members and soldiers from the walled defenses?

Saved!

She obviously plied her trade for money. Did she invest herself in the main religious cult of Jericho? Probably. But something turned her cravings to a new source of nourishment. By the time the spies met her in Joshua 2, this is what she was whispering: "I know that the Lord has given this land to you and that a great fear of you has fallen on us... for the Lord your God is God in heaven above and on the earth below!" (Joshua 2:8,11).

Thus, when Rahab changed allegiance in the affairs of her society, it was a religious thing. Obviously this is what Salmon saw in her when he observed the way she lived among the Israelites after Jericho was destroyed.

So did Jesus. That's why he was proud to point to his great-grandmother's picture in the family photo album.

38

The Living Dead

"As the body without the spirit is dead, so faith without deeds is dead." (James 2:26)

For those who inquire into the strange religion of voodoo the zombie is the most sinister feature. Tradition has it that dead bodies can be brought back to life by magical rites. These "zombies" are then employed as slaves, little more than a virtual "skeleton crew" labor force.

Zombies are actually created when atrophine, a poison found in the juices of the thorn apple, is secretly fed to the enemies of the local chieftain of black magic. Though the person soon appears to die, a kind of life lingers in the circulatory system. After the funeral and burial, those in the employ of the voodoo priest dig up the body and revive the physical shell enough to create the living dead. Intellectually, spiritually, and volitionally comatose, these zombies stumble about only at the whim of their masters.

TV Times

The practice of voodoo is alive and well in Haiti yet today. Beyond the shores of that island nation there have also been reports of similar strange occurrences. Several years ago a father in London, England, told a juvenile court that his 16-year-old son was not responsible for his recent acts of random vandalism. According to the father, the lad had done nothing but lounge in front of the television for nearly eight months. Said the father, the boy "has been reduced to the state of a zombie." Couch potatoes beware!

Of course, the Christian Church has known about zombies for centuries. In Revelation 3 Jesus said to the folks in the Sardis congregation, "I know... you have a reputation of being alive, but you are dead!" Sounds like the creature-feature *Night of the Living Dead* might have been filmed there!

In some ways the spiritual mix that makes zombies in the church is far more sinister than the poisonous atrophine of voodoo. James says the transformation happens not because we ingest some poisonous faith-killer but when we sit on our hands! When we first believe in God faith is not so much *taught* as it is *caught*—we see how it drives and energizes the actions of a friend and we crave the same for ourselves. It is a similar process that unfolds when we lose faith: belief seeps away through the atrophy of our unflexed spiritual muscles. Our religion is not challenged to death, but rather relaxed into oblivion.

Softened To Death

A youngster I knew some years ago wanted so much to have pet goldfish that he finally wheedled his mom into getting the basic equipment of aquatic ranching. Following the usual scenario in these matters, after a month and a half the two little swimmers had died. When the lad came crying to his mother, she followed him to observe the disaster in a bowl. The goldfish were sort of falling apart and a big cloud of mush washed through the bowl.

"What happened?" the mother asked.

"Well," he replied, "when I changed their water I wanted them to be comfortable, so I put in some of that softener in the laundry room."

He had softened the fish to death! Atrophine makes zombies. Atrophy rots muscles. And spiritual atrophy happens when faith is not exercised.

How will you strengthen the muscles of your religion today?

39

Teachers' Trials

"Not many of you should presume to be teachers, my brothers, because you know that we who teach will be judged more strictly." (James 3:1)

A boy in first grade came home from school and told his mother that his class had had a substitute teacher. "What was her name?" asked the mother, but the young lad couldn't remember.

Since she knew most of the regular substitutes from her time of serving on the school board, the mother asked, "Was she a young woman or an older woman?"

The boy thought for a moment and then replied, "I don't know. She looked brand new to me."

Combat Pay

Teaching is not an easy profession. Maurine Mugleston remembers the time she stood at rink side watching a hockey game. One of the players rammed into the board and was immediately crushed by two burley men from the other team, each lashing out for the puck. When they bounced off him, the first player wobbled on his skates and then slid to the ice, knocking his head. Pushing himself up, his nose dripping blood, he saw Maurine standing there. "There must be an easier way to make a living," he roared to her.

"I'll trade jobs!" she shouted back.

"What do you do?"

"I teach sixth grade 6," she replied.

"Forget it!" he said, and was gone.

From earliest recorded history teachers have been killed (Socrates), banished (Damien), burned at the stake (Hus), vilified (Scopes), and assaulted (Sullivan). An elementary school teacher, realizing the weight of her profession, once said her job was to take hold of a bunch of "live wires and see that they are well-grounded." Those with queasy stomachs need not apply!

Holy Ground

Yet it is not the danger of the teaching profession that causes James to issue his stern warning. Rather, it is the mindset of arrogance and superiority often latent in the teaching posture itself. Nick Boeke found his four-year-old daughter standing before her dolls, all lined up on the couch, one day. When he asked her what she was doing, she replied, "I'm playing school. I'm the teacher and these are all my prisoners!"

Teachers stand over their pupils by default. The profession, by its very nature, projects people into unequal roles. Some are able to use their dominant roles to nurture the best out of others. But when some teachers take advantage of their status in order to intimidate, violence is born. That's where James' caution takes effect: those who presume a stance of pedagogue had better be certain that they do not crush bruised reeds or snuff out glowing embers among those they instruct.

A distinguished Oxford don had a particular way of snubbing clever young undergraduates. He would invite a student to accompany him on a long walk, leaving it to the other to begin conversation. Since the silence would eventually embarrass the student, he usually would blubber out something trite. Immediately the professor would pounce on the banal remark and destroy the student's psyche.

One student received his summons to the ordeal, and had heard others tell of the inevitable outcome. He decided not to say anything until spoken to, regardless of the inner turmoil he might be fighting. Finally the professor was obliged to start. "They tell me you're clever, Smith," he said, hoping to unnerve his pupil into a no-win corner. "Is that so?"

"Yes," replied F. E. Smith, future British attorney general. The don was duffed, and the conversation ended with further embarrassed silence. The old man had made a mockery of his profession, and rightly deserved these turned tables.

Reward

If the penalty against teachers is increased, so also is the reward for faithfulness. When Dr. Chanrasekhar was a professor at the University of Chicago in 1947, he was scheduled to teach an advanced seminar in astrophysics. At the time he was living in Wisconsin, doing research at the Yerkes astronomical observatory. When only two students registered for his class, the administration advised him to cancel the seminar.

He, however, felt an obligation to respond to the call of the two. So he made the more than 100 mile round trip every day, all winter long. Ten years later those two students, Chen Ning Yang and Tsung-Dao Lee both won the Nobel prize for physics. And in 1983, so did Dr. Chandrasekhar.

Said Robert Schmidgall: "We teach what we know; we reproduce what we are." Only when the students are honorable may the teacher be honored.

The New Testament calls that discipleship. And the Master is graded by others on the quality of our reflection of him.

40

Absolute Truths

"We all stumble in many ways. If anyone is never at fault in what he says, he is a perfect man, able to keep his whole body in check." (James 3:2)

In Susan Howatch's novel *Absolute Truths* the main character is a rather perfect man. Oh, to be sure, Charles Ashworth had his little peculiarities in his younger years and he needed the guidance of Jon Darrow to help him understand himself. But all in all he is a portrait of humanity at its best—sound and sleek in body, steady in temperament, keen in intellect, faithful in relationships, and unwavering in morality. He is the consummate churchman. It is no accident of fate that has placed him in the high post of Bishop of Starbridge.

Magnificent Suffering

Just as he faces off against those in the church and society who seem to be changing the morals of culture, his wife suddenly dies of a blood clot in the brain. Charles is with her at the time and watches in horrified helplessness as she slumps lifeless to the floor.

Bishop Ashworth's world is shattered. Still, no one will hold him accountable for his depression and excessive drinking since these are the normal temporary responses to such a loss. He is still a perfect man, perfect even in his grief.

Then, as he finally clears their bedroom of his wife's clothes and cosmetics, Charles discovers her journal. For some years she had been penning her secret thoughts. It began as an attempt at prayer, providing a means by which Mrs. Asworth tried to sort through the turmoil inside in order to present herself to God honestly.

Cracks in the Paint

Some of the pages of the journal retrace the minutia of life—meetings and schedules, changing seasons, weather and fashions. Woven throughout, however, is a remarkable analysis of Charles' own psyche. He was not aware that she knew him so perceptively. More than that, he did not realize that there were flaws in his own character that kept her and their two sons at a (dis)respectful distance. Formally his life was in tune with the "absolute truths" of Christian behavior. Yet somewhere in the firmness of his propriety he had failed to grasp the one essential absolute truth of God: it is grace that drives love, and not pedantic obedience.

Here is the greatest rub for those who are mature in life and faith. It is so easy to presume that strength of character and moral uprightness are the goals of faith and life. Certainly they are admirable, and obedience to God is a high value.

Flying Lessons

But there is something about love that stands just above them. A dear friend once explained it like this: in a dream he saw a marvelous apparatus of yellow silk billowing in the breezes next to a cliff. It was a transportation device of some kind, though he couldn't see either engines or supports. Like a magical tent, it floated in space.

Inside was a man whose face seemed so familiar and friendly my friend knew immediately that this was an intimate acquaintance. However, he could not seem to remember how they were associated nor the man's name. The man, with a smile of warmth, invited him to step off the cliff into the contrivance and be carried on a delightful journey in the yellow tent.

But my friend was so intrigued by the device itself that he wanted to try it on his own. *He* wanted to pilot the magical airship. So when he entered the craft he fought the man for control and pushed him out onto the cliff. Unfortunately, just as my friend felt the power of flight swell in his commanding grasp, the entire yellow tent began to collapse in on itself and plummet to disaster below. No matter what he did, my friend could not make the "machine" fly. He cried out for help, and suddenly the man he had pushed out reappeared at his side. In that exact moment the airship began to billow and slow its freefall. Soon they were soaring together.

Without a further thought my friend knew that the strangely familiar man was Jesus. He also knew why Jesus said to him, "Don't you know that the power to fly is not found in the 'machine' nor in your skills as a pilot but in me?"

If someone close to me were to pen a secret study of my life, I wonder if they would be able to detect that "absolute truth" expressed.

41

Bit Wit

"When we put bits into the mouths of horses to make them obey us, we can turn the whole animal. Or take ships as an example. Although they are so large and are driven by strong winds, they are steered by a very small rudder wherever the pilot wants to go. Likewise the tongue is a small part of the body, but it makes great boasts." (James 3:3-5)

When French novelist Tristan Bernard stepped into a Parisian horse carriage one day, the horse started suddenly. It reared and kicked, pawing the air with its front hoofs and dancing madly. As the driver attempted to bring it under control, a single energized spasm shot through its body and, after a moment of rigid stretching, it fell over on its side.

Bernard climbed down from the carriage and said politely to the coachman, "Is that all the tricks he knows?"

Tricky Terror

Very likely the driver was even more surprised by the horse's behavior than was Bernard. To paraphrase a proverb, "Who can know the mind of a horse?"

Recently my wife and daughters spent an afternoon riding horses. All went well until the girth strap came loose on one of the saddles. In something like slow motion, one of our daughters gradually tipped to the side as she rode along until gravity pulled her to the ground. Her horse was a little skittish after that, she said, and much less responsive to the bit and reins than before. Of course!

It doesn't always take a fright to separate between the wills of horse and rider, however. The last time I pretended equestrian skills was on a trail ride. The horse knew the way much better than me, and was also very certain where he didn't want to go. No matter how I tried to use them, all my commands were very ineffectual.

Power Play

The bit in a horse's mouth is meant to link the mind of the rider with that of the beast. When it works well there is a beautiful display of equestrian grace and elegance. But when communication breaks down, two passions vie for dominance and horse is usually stronger than human.

Control can be an ugly word, particularly where it demeans and diminishes or where it clubs and coerces. But a good rider's control over his mount is the key to having both experience the best of horsemanship. So also in communication. Our passions, wild and delightful as they are when they carry us away in strength or ecstasy, are fierce mounts to ride. Sometimes we want them to go out of control and we dance with abandon or shout with fear or cheer with mob madness.

Reining In

But there are passions within that should not escape the heart's stable without a sound bridle and a rigid bit. It is the angry passions that fight control to our hurt and others' harm. Angry people throw stupid words and heavy fists. Angry drivers yell nasty slogans, waving all the while with a single finger. Angry spouses scream feelings better left unspoken, and find the jousting tournament has left one or the other maimed or dead inside.

A friend of mine who was quite pleased with his flapping tongue often told people proudly that he had "diarrhea of the mouth." As long as he could connect his tongue with meaningful insights the stream was tolerable. But, by his own confession, his brain logged off at 10 p.m. each night while his tongue kept rattling. An unbridled tongue was not a good thing for him to boast about.

It shouldn't be for anyone, says James.

42

Raging Fires and Refreshing Fluids

"Consider what a great forest is set on fire by a small spark. The tongue also is a fire, a world of evil among the parts of the body. It corrupts the whole person, sets the whole course of his life on fire, and is itself set on fire by hell." (James 3:5-6)

One of our daughters went to an all day youth event some years ago. Besides mediocre food and boring "motivational" talks there was also an afternoon of games and recreation. Our daughter got into the line-up for the Sumo Wrestlers. She is only a petite little thing, but when they swallowed up her body in the foam rubber Sumo wrestler suit she looked like Fat Albert. The point of the Sumo wrestling contest was to topple over the other pint-sized person bouncing around inside a similar suit. Both people were so clumsy they looked hysterically funny. And both were so padded that they couldn't hurt each other if they wanted to.

Padded Hearts

When I watched those playtime Sumo wrestlers it reminded me of what the Bible says about patience and kindness. People who are patient seem to have a high capacity to absorb lots of the hurtful stuff that is always bouncing around in the daily grind of living. It is almost as if they regularly wear extra padding in order not to get quickly riled.

That does not necessarily make them insensitive, but it does help control the anger that rages through society. Angry people throw fists. Angry drivers cut you off and wave at you with one finger. Angry athletes smash equipment, and sometimes bodies. Angry men beat up on women. Angry women slap children. Angry nations strut military hardware and everyone cowers in fear.

We protect ourselves as best we can from the anger of others. We develop "civilization" in order to bring the darker passions under some rational control. But our tongues seem to be outside the loop on that rewiring and the bullets we fire from our mouths pass right through the protection of other padded hearts.

A Handful of Options

While we cannot make other people behave better, there is something we can do about our own stance in the Sumo wrestling of life. Someone taught me long ago that there are only five basic responses we can make to others when they direct conversation, good or ill, toward us. These five "punches" are *evaluate, instruct, support, probe,* and *understand.* When we evaluate the other person's speech or actions, we set ourselves up as judge over her. When we instruct, we lift our position to that of teacher. When we express support, we approach the other person as friend. When we probe we seek further engagement, and bring the person into our hearts. And when we summarize and repeat what he's said, we show him that we understand.

On the surface this may seem like a conversational word game, and for some people it turns out to be merely that. For most of us, unfortunately, it is a game we need to begin playing with earnestness if we would hope to improve our communication and get that tongue off the hurtful trigger.

You see, evaluative and instructional responses in conversation tend to shut down communication and throw barbs into the other person's soul. While none of us believes we ever use those rejoinders unless truly called for, the fact of research is that typical North American conversation includes around 80% of evaluative and instructional statements! In other words, we are almost constantly blowing pricks

137

right through the Sumo wrestlers' padding of other people. More tragically, most of the time we don't even know it.

The Stuff of Society

Yet that seems to be what society encourages and normal and proper behavior. It certainly seems to play best in political campaigns, and why Jews and Arabs need guns in the Middle East, or racial tensions breed unchecked in a dozen other hot spots around the globe.

Often in our homes it is the same thing. A husband shakes an angry fist of paper at his wife and shouts, "Look at these bills! Where do you think the money's going to come from?" But he's not asking a question. He's really saying, "Oh you stupid woman!" A moody teen yells at her parents, "Why are you always riding my case?" and the air is supercharged for a fight. Church members quibble about practices and raise their doctrinal swords to kill those who look most like themselves.

Bridge Builders

Maybe someday the raging fires of hell will be quenched by the refreshing fluids of heaven. James hopes that it will begin in the church. And, indeed, sometimes it does. Palmer Ofuoku, a Nigerian pastor, remembers when the first missionaries came to his village. Some few became Christians, but not many, because these pale ones spoke many words of judgment (*evaluation*) and demand (*instruction*). It wasn't until another missionary came that Ofuoku began to listen and respond with faith and care. Why? Because, said pastor Ofuoku, this man stayed next to me when I was sick (*support*). He asked me about my family (*probing*), and let me know that he genuinely cared about me (*understanding*). Said Palmer Ofuoku, "He built a bridge of friendship to me, and Jesus walked across."

I wonder how many bridges like that I've built lately.

43

Talk *Isn't* Cheap

"All kinds of animals, birds, reptiles and creatures of the sea are being tamed and have been tames by man, but no man can tame the tongue. It is a restless evil, full of deadly poison. With the tongue we praise our Lord and Father, and with it we curse men, who have been made in God's likeness. Out of the same mouth come praise and cursing. My brothers, this should not be. Can both fresh water and salt water flow from the same spring? My brothers, can a fig tree bear olives, or a grapevine bear figs? Neither can a salt spring produce fresh water." (James 3:7-12)

A Jewish rabbi was officiating at the funeral of a woman from his congregation. During the service her husband constantly shook his head back and forth. In a low and mournful sob he kept repeating, over and over: "I love her! I love her! I love her..."

After the burial, the man refused to leave the gravesite. People tried to take his arm and lead him back to his car but he shrugged off every attempt. Finally the rabbi himself made the effort. He said, "It's time to go now, Fred. You can take your memories with you."

Only then did the sorrow break out with explanation. Fred shook his head again and sobbed: "You don't understand! I loved her so much but I never let her know it! I never told her how much she meant to me!"

The Sounds of Silence

It was a sorry sight, said the rabbi. The worst part was that this man had stood in his congregation every Shabbat for years, intoning the praises of God. Yet this tongue so skilled in religious testimony had missed a thousand opportunities to declare what was desperately needed in the most important relationship of his earthly life.

We all know the poison that tongues can produce when wagging incessantly. But there is also a poison of silence. We can waste our words on tedious talk that babbles of weather and horsepower and clothes and customs, and forget to make the sounds of love. A university study found that a typical North American father converses with each of his children an average of 37 seconds per day. There's not a lot that can be said in that time. Very likely for many of us even many of those seconds are spent collecting communication miscues that bite rather than words that heal and offer hope.

Talking to the Photo Album

Richard Leigh remembers well how a lifetime of neighboring in the same house still left members of a single family wandering past each other as total strangers. His words became a haunting reflection:

The greatest man I never knew lived just down the hall,

And every day we said "Hello!" but never touched at all.

He was in his paper; I was in my room;

How was I to know he thought I hung the moon?

The greatest man I never knew came home late every night.

He never had too much to say; too much was on his mind.

I never really knew him, and now it seems so sad...

Everything he gave to us took all he had.

Then the days turned into years, and the memories to black and white.

He grew cold like an old winter wind blowing across my life.

The greatest words I never heard I guess I'll never hear.

The man I thought could never die has been dead almost a year.

I hear he was good at business, but there was a business left to do.

He never said he loves me... Guess he thought I knew.

Most of us know when the barbs of our tongues dig blood from the souls of others. But few of us are wise enough to hear the pain caused by silence when we poison some of our best relationships by saying too little of words that encourage and engage and build and heal.

44

Wisdom in Winnipeg

"Who is wise and understanding among you? Let him show it by his good life, by deeds done in the humility that comes from wisdom." (James 3:13)

Fred Craddock once flew to Winnipeg, Manitoba, to speak at a church conference. Unfortunately his arrival coincided with the worst snowstorm of the decade. When no one picked him up at the airport, Fred found a taxi willing to brave the whiteouts and drifts in the drive required to get him to his motel. There a message awaited him; he was to call the man who booked him for the conference.

"I'm sorry, Fred," said the man. "We didn't count on this blizzard. We've had to cancel the conference. In fact, we're so snowed in here at the church that we can't even get out there to the motel to pick you up for a meal. You're on your own."

Sanctuary

The motel was not all that great. It didn't even have a restaurant. When Fred called the office to find directions to some food place nearby, a woman suggested the coffee shop at the bus depot. It was about a block and a half away. Battling gale force winds and stinging snow, it still took Fred twenty minutes to stumble over there.

The bus depot was dirty. The coffee shop was worse. Even so, an overflow crowd had taken refuge inside its steamy windows. Everyone seemed to know the plight of those who newly entered, for when Fred saw no seats open kind strangers at a booth shoved over to make space. Soon he was eating a tasteless gray soup.

The door opened again. This time a woman struggled to find her way into the throng. Her lingered entry brought out the man with the greasy apron. "Hey!" he yelled. "Close that door! You're letting all the cold air in here!"

Like Fred, the woman had to find sanctuary at a table of strangers. When the man with the greasy apron walked over and asked what she wanted, she asked for a glass of water. He returned and asked again, "What do you want?"

"The water will be fine," she said.

Snobbery

"No," replied the man. "What do you want to order from the menu?"

"I'm really not hungry," she answered. "I'll just stick with the water."

"Look lady!" came the response. "We've got paying customers waiting! If you're not going to order anything, you'll have to get out!"

"Can't I just stay a few minutes and get warmed up?" she asked.

"No way!" he said. "If you don't want to order, you'll have to leave!"

So the woman gathered herself and stood to make an exit. Of course, these two had gotten the attention of everyone in the room. As the woman rose, everyone noticed the men on either side of her pushing back their chairs and standing as well. And the men next to them. In a flash, everyone at that table stood and turned to leave, plates still bulging with food. Something like an electric current buzzed through the room, and all at once everyone else got up and moved toward the door.

Solidarity

The man with the greasy apron was startled. "All right! All right!" he said, motioning everyone to sit again. "She can stay!" He even brought her a bowl of soup.

As Fred turned back to his own bowl of broth he found that it tasted better than he remembered. In fact, it reminded him of something but he could not quite recall what. He turned to the stranger next to him and asked, "Do you know her?"

"No," said the man. "Never saw her before. But if she can't sit here to get warm, I wouldn't want to stay in a place like this."

As Fred paused to leave a short while later it finally dawned on him that what he had been thinking about when the soup gained its taste was the last time he shared the sacrament of communion. Maybe these mixed strangers in search of shelter were only a pack of isolated bodies. But for a moment the spirit of Jesus warmed the air in the room and they breathed in something of the wisdom James urged.

45

The Killer Virus

"But if you harbor bitter envy and selfish ambition in your hearts, do not boast about it or deny the truth. Such 'wisdom' does not come down from heaven but is earthly, unspiritual, of the devil. For where you have envy and selfish ambition, there you find disorder and every evil practice." (James 3:14-16)

My friend and I just had a contest to see which of us is more holy. I won because I'm more humble than he is.

Of course I'm being facetious. But we did have a rather interesting conversation about piety, ministry, and the pitfalls of trying always to lead people deeper into spirituality and expressions of Christian living. Every step of "success" I might have as a pastor breeds new polyps of cancerous envy and selfish ambition. Last night a young lad in our church looked up at me and said, "You know God, don't you?" He said it with all the innocent awe that a six-year-old can intone.

I said yes to him and then asked him if he knew God. "Not like you do," he replied. If only he understood how hard it is to be close to God and at the same time to be all wrapped up in the skin of envy and selfish ambition. I want to preach great sermons so that people's hearts will be moved and stirred, so that children will believe in God, so that men will deepen their devotion and women will express great faith. At the same time I want to preach great sermons so that people will say what a great preacher I am.

Greatness

When I listen to other preachers preach, they always have powerful things to say. They talk so clearly and cleverly to their congregations. They shine with grace and cry with hearts broken for the things of God. And I'm envious. When I see loving pastors touch people with grace and kindness, knowing how to listen and when to say just the right things, I'd like to be like them. In fact, I'd like to be better than them so that people would come to me instead. When I visit those mega-churches shaped by great leaders who seems to know exactly how God wants to build the Kingdom, I wish they would turn to me and say, "Wayne, you're a successful pastor. What should we do next? Tell us how you built up your church."

I know what James means by selfish ambition and envy. I wish I didn't, but I do. John Adams, the second president of the United States, wrote this in his diary as a young man: "How shall I gain a reputation? How shall I spread an opinion of myself as a lawyer of distinguished genius, learning, and virtue?" Sometimes, in my crassest moments, I wonder the same. When will people take note of me? When will I get my "fifteen minutes of fame," as Andy Warhol put it?

Grief

I'm not obsessed with these thoughts. I don't dwell on them, and these passions don't rule my life. At least I don't think so. But that is the insidiousness of sin, isn't it? It uses every grace and gift we might have from God, turning each into a competitive contestant in a public game show race toward those very goals we know are so good. When we achieve some spiritual success by these pushy means, the reward is cruel and the prize is much more ugly than we had imagined.

J. C. Penney, whose stores are now a major marketing force in North America, remembered working for six dollars a week at Joslin's Dry Goods Store in Denver. He was ambitious, and craved the day when he would be worth $100,000. As wealth poured in and he met that initial goal, he said that the old exhilaration wore off and he had to rekindle the driving passions by setting his sights at becoming a millionaire. He and his wife worked even harder to expand the business. Then one day she caught cold and developed pneumonia. In a short while she was dead. "When she died," he said, "my world crashed about me. To build a business, to make a success in the eyes of men, to accumulate money -- what was the purpose of life? I felt mocked by life..."

Grace

Why does it so often take a death in the family to wake us up to life's truest values, and to perform surgery on the cancers of sin that grow within? No one really knows. In fact, God probably asked himself that very question on the first Good Friday.

46

Pure Wisdom

"But the wisdom that comes from heaven is first of all pure...." (James 3:17)

Brenda and I were waiting to be seated at a dinner theater. The couple next to us kept looking in our direction, whispering with raised eyebrows of seeming recognition. Finally we stumbled into that first awkward contact, and in less time than it takes to plant a tulip bulb we knew people they knew, and they connected with places we had been.

Buddies

Suddenly we were pals, old friends, intimate confidants. That was when he decided to let us in on a few business insights. Soon he was sharing more information than we really wanted to know: racial slurs, shady ways to use other people's possessions, theological judgments on those who did not agree with his views. While all his business sense ran along highways of truth, it consistently veered into moral neighborhoods we did not want to visit.

As I listened to his pitch I felt prickles of dislike needling me. I think it was because the valuable wisdom he offered was packaged in cheap tinsel and gaudy wrap that made it look very ugly. It reminded me of the horribly funny scene in the movie *Trainspotting* where the main character loses something precious down a toilet in a foul restroom (the sign says "THE DIRTIEST IN ALL OF SCOTLAND"). He ends

148

up forcing himself through the putrid plumbing and swimming an ocean of disgusting sewage in order to recover the prize.

The incongruity bites, doesn't it?

Business

When Erik Eriksen wrote his famous biography of Martin Luther he observed that all of us endure similar experiences of life, but that what makes some people special is their ability to ferret out their truest selves through those adventures. In Luther's case it became a matter of *"Greatness Finding Itself,"* and that's what Eriksen titled his study.

Eriksen said that one of the main crises of life was the quest to hang onto integrity. It is very hard, he said, for us to keep ourselves together. Even though we are mostly good people, we tend to break little pieces of our hearts off here and there, thinking we will serve some greater good in the long run. We may never destroy ourselves in some heinous crime or gross violation of decency. Still we frazzle the edges of our souls through compromise in a dozen minor matters.

Take, for example, the letter I received this morning. A man writes: "I was earning a good living as a lawyer, but as anyone in the legal profession will tell you there is a lot of stress that comes with the job." So he explained a "get rich quick" scheme that robbed those lower down on a multiplying pyramid. Then he gloated that he made millions in three months without ever lifting a finger. He invited others to participate in his venture, keeping just this side of illegality by riding a loop of moral slipperiness between two civil codes.

He is not hurting anybody, is he? Since the government will never be able to prosecute him for criminal activity, why not share the greasy cash with him?

In fact, why not do a thousand things that are pushed at us in the language of our times? And why not follow your desires or your passions or your heart, as long as you come out a winner?

Beauty

Well, if James is right, all wisdoms are not the same. Some are not pure. In other words, they fracture our selves rather than keep us congruent with life in its essential character. One of our daughters' caused that to jump out at me recently. She wanted to go on a particular outing with her friends, but circumstances prevented her from participating the fund-raising activities necessary to make it happen. So she stomped and blustered that she was not going. She said she did not want to go anymore, even when we offered to do other things to help her. "No!" she yelled. "I won't go!"

When I asked her why, she just said, "It's not right. That's not the way it's supposed to happen."

What does she know? She knows some wisdom that comes from heaven. In the forming years of her delicate heart, she realizes something that many of us tend to rush past in the hardness of our years: you cannot rewrite the rules of life and still connect with God or find yourself whole.

47

Peace-Loving Wisdom

"But the wisdom that comes from heaven is first of all pure; then peace-loving...." (James 3:17)

For many years our family sponsored a child in Africa through the Compassion International assistance organization. We began doing this when we returned from our term of missionary service in Nigeria. Since our girls were all very young while we lived in Africa, we were certain that they would soon forget their playmates. We thought that by corresponding with an African "sister" they would grow in their appreciation for some of the culture they left behind when we moved back to North America.

Hategekimana

Our first African "child" was a young girl named Hategekimana. She lived in Rwanda. Her picture was prominently displayed in our home. Our daughters sent her little gifts when they celebrated their birthdays. We eagerly read her translated letters when they arrived in the mail, and sent her notes of encouragement and appreciation.

In the early 1990's social violence reared and spat in Rwanda. The majority Hutus struck in vengeance against the ruling Tutsis. In a matter of months the soils of Rwanda were washed with blood, and our Hategekimana disappeared. A note came from Compassion officials, one day, describing the torment and anguish ripping at the country. All expatriate personnel had been evacuated, and it might be months before anyone could re-enter Rwanda. They hoped, with us, that Hategekimana would survive.

We prayed for peace. We prayed for Hategekimana and her family. Yet when the Compassion officials risked their lives to return, Hategekimana was nowhere to be found. Did she die in battle? Was her house burned around her? Is she a nameless refugee in the camps of Zaire and Burundi? Quite possibly we will never know. Hategekimana is gone. We still pray for her and her family at our meal table. But none of us has hope any longer that she will be found.

Without Hategekimana we might easily have ignored the pain of Africa. After all, the violence there was a world apart from our secure isolation. But she brought it home to us. She made us understand again the measure of John Donne's verse: "No man is an Island, entire of it self; every man is a piece of the Continent, a part of the main; if a clod be washed away by the sea, Europe is the less, as well as if a promontory were, as well as if a manor of thy friends or of thine own were; any man's death diminishes me, because I am involved in Mankind; And therefore never send to know for whom the bell tolls; It tolls for thee" (*Meditation XVII*).

The "Red Girl"

To us Hategekimana is like that patch of red in Steven Spielberg's powerful film, *Schindler's List*. Spielberg wanted to personalize the pain of the Jewish people in the Warsaw ghetto who were rounded up like frightened lambs and herded to carts of slaughter. The movie was filmed in the haunting shades of gray, somewhere between the hope of white and the despair of black. In this particular scene, however, where the camera panned back to show the global scope of hell erupting on these people from street to street and block to block, Spielberg caught our attention and kept us spellbound by painting one faint spot of color. He brushed in the swatch of red fabric of one young girl's coat. While the horrors raged and the people ran, our eyes were fixed on this rosy cipher. We watched her get tangled in a mob rushing hopelessly this way and that. We saw her telltale coat peeking from behind a brick corner in a useless attempt at hiding. We picked her image out of a crowd being mowed down with furious fire from

Nazi guns. And then we wept when her little red form was tossed onto a cart for disposal with the rest of the "garbage" removed from the street the next day.

Sometimes the news desensitizes us to the pain of violence. We become spectators of wars on television. We hear words about murder happening to people we do not know. We read studies documenting brutality and abuse among families living in other cities. From the immunity of our recliners we surf through the channels to find something fun and entertaining, and thank God for our "peace" and "safety."

Prince of Peace

But isolation is not peace. James does not tell us to ask for ignorance. Instead, he instructs us to pray for wisdom. The wisdom that comes from above. The wisdom that brought the "Prince of Peace" to wrestle with the powers of violence, and to allow them to spend themselves in hurt upon him.

Why?

Because he knows Hategekimana by name, and he will not stay in the isolation of heaven until she is found safe in the care of her Father and his Family. Just read the telltale splotches of red that he paints across grayness of human history.

48

Considerate Wisdom

"But the wisdom that comes from heaven is first of all pure; then peace-loving, considerate...." (James

3:17)

Cecil Rhodes, the nineteenth century expansionist South African statesman and financier, was known for his precise manners and impeccable dress code. Yet he wore his social correctness with a considerate heart. For example, when Rhodes was hosting a formal dinner at his Kimberley home, one of the guests was unable to arrive until the very moment of seating. He had no time to change his travel-stained and rumpled clothes.

The young man's obvious discomfort in this company of glittering women and dapper gentlemen was made more acute because Rhodes, usually so punctual, delayed his appearance at the table. The dusty fellow felt like pig in a hen house, surrounded by clucking criticism.

Graciousness

But when Rhodes finally entered the room to greet his guests and begin the meal, they were taken aback. Rather than sporting formal attire, he was clad in a shabby old blue suit! Now it was the young man's turn to feel at ease while the others wondered at their being over-dressed.

Only the household servants ever knew the whole story. Rhodes had been descending the stairs as the last guest arrived. Noting his travel-weary look, Rhodes had returned to his dressing room, removed his black tuxedo, and quickly slipped into the sorriest suit he could find in his closet. It was his way of politely declaring the misfit to be welcome at his table.

Cecil Rhodes had class.

While we would all commend "considerateness" as valuable social grace, it is interesting that James elevates it to the level of divine wisdom. What makes it so?

Goodness

Maybe it has to do with the fact that a considerate person takes thought of others. Will Durant, the famous philosopher and historian, was asked for advice by one of his grandchildren. He summarized all his wisdom in "ten commandments." At the heart of them is this advice: "Do not speak while another is speaking. Discuss, do not dispute. Absorb and acknowledge whatever truth you can find in opinions different from your own. Be courteous and considerate to all, especially to those who oppose you."

We would all like to have friends like that. Certainly we expect God to treat us that way.

But maybe "considerateness" is more than just thoughtfulness. Stan Wiersma, writing under his pen name "Sietze Buning," explored the religious roots of being considerate in his collection of folk poetry titled *Style and Class* (Middleburg Press, 1982). Much of what we display in life, said Sietze Buning, has to do with "style"—we watch how others dress or act, and then we try to imitate those we admire. But "class" is living out of the nobility of your inner character, said Sietze.

He tells this little story to illustrate what he means:

Queen Wilhelmina was entertaining the

Frisian Cattle Breeders' Association at dinner.

The Frisian farmers didn't know what to make of their finger bowls.

They drank them down.

155

The stylish courtiers from the Hague nudged each other,

and pointed, and laughed at such lack of style.

Until the queen herself, without a smile, raised her finger bowl and drained it,

obliging all the courtiers to follow suit, without a smile. (p. 17)

Sietze Buning ends with this note of judgment:

The courtiers had style, but Queen Wilhelmina had class.

Grace

While that makes for good story telling, Sietze Buning takes it one surprising step further. He links style to the wisdom of the world and class to the wisdom of heaven. The former tries to get us to fit in with the right crowd, looking the right way and eating the right foods, while driving the right vehicles. That's style.

But class – *real* class – happens to us when we realize that we are children of God. If God is King, we are nobility—Princesses and Princes in the realm of the great ruler!

Children of the King do not need to prove themselves, nor do they need to flaunt their status. If they have learned well at home the true worth of their lives, they can treat others with courtesy and respect. They can be considerate.

It is a religious thing. It is also the best kind of wisdom.

49

Submissive Wisdom

"But the wisdom that comes from heaven is first of all pure; then peace-loving, considerate,

submissive...." (James 3:17)

During the heated times of the Reformation, when Martin Luther and Ulrich Zwingli were exchanging strong words about biblical interpretations and ecclesiastical practices, Zwingli spent a troubled morning walking the mountain trails of his beloved Switzerland. From a distance he observed two goats making their way in opposite directions on a path barely stitched to the side of a cliff. It was obvious that not even these nimble creatures would be able to negotiate past one another as they met.

Zwingli watched them round a corner and come face to face. There was a moment of uncertainty as each feinted a power move at the other. Both goats took several steps backward, and set hind legs in a posture of attack. In a surprise twist, however, the goat at the lower level suddenly collapsed onto the narrow ledge until the other goat could walk quickly over its back. Then each danced on.

Zwingli was impressed. Here was strength defined by submission. It allowed two opponents to survive a little crisis in order to get on with the larger dimensions of their lives. Zwingli considered this moment a divine parable, and brought it into his next encounter with Luther.

Rising by Serving

Submission is a crucial dimension of spiritual wisdom that has few advocates in a society strong on personal assertion. John Maxwell, in his book *Developing the Leader within You* (Nelson, 1993), noted that there are five different levels of authority that a person can attain in life, but each is based on an increasing willingness to submit to outside forces or influences.

The first is "position," where people are challenged to respect you for your rank in society. Second, there is the authority of "permission" that happens when you enter a relationship of significance with someone else, and that person allows you to have a say in his affairs. Third comes the authority of "production" in which you are honored for the results you can get. Fourth, there is the authority of "people development" which recognizes the empowerment you have given others. Finally comes the quality of "personhood" where the very character of your life demands respect.

We can all name people who gather one or another of these forms of authority to themselves: a judge, for instance, fits the first; a dating partner the second; my neighbor across the street did such a good job of bringing up the production in his factory in our town that he was transferred to tackle the development of an even larger plant in another state—that is an example of number three; my uncle who retired as a high school guidance counselor got the accolades of the fourth; and we only have to say names like "Billy Graham" and "Mother Teresa" to explore the last.

As a Parent

Interestingly, the source of all five of these forms of authority exists in our relationship with our parents. A mother has position over us when we are young children. She can abuse that position, as some have, or she can also use it to give us a wholesome sense of ourselves, as many others have.

A father has our permission, early in life, to direct and guide us. We go looking for support and advise from him. A mother holds over us the authority of production. Before we can tie our shoes or dress ourselves, she is doing things for us we could not begin to handle on our own. So it is with level four—a good parent is able to serve in developing our characters. When we sat around at my Grandmother's funeral, some years ago, my dad and all his siblings said the same thing: "Mom always believed in us. She always prayed for us. We wouldn't be the people we are without her care."

In fact, when all these forms of authority are rolled up in a single package it is that fifth form, the one that is particularly hard to earn, which epitomizes the best of what great parenting is about. There is no higher tribute that can be paid a person than to say that he was a father to me, or she was like my own mother. In our brief years of life, as we meander through strange and familiar paths, both untried and yet as ancient as time itself, no one can help us find our truest selves better than a wise and loving parent.

This is the mystery of submission. The best of ourselves rarely comes when we fight it out on our own. Instead, it is brought to life when someone who loves me takes my hand and helps me to reach higher than I thought I could.

Harnessing the Will

The ancients always compared our wills to horses. It is a fitting comparison, I think. There is a stallion inside each of us, snorting and restless, and nervously pacing. That energy and strength of character can be thrown about with the destructive power of a mad horse that will not be mastered, or it can be harnessed by a rider and a bit, and channeled into speed and purpose and direction.

Your will is strong. You need it to survive. But you also need it to be brought under submission to a higher power if you would be fully human. Maybe it begins in our relationship with our parents. But it finds its fullness, as James notes, when we get wise in faith and submit to One who said, "My yoke is easy and my burden is light" (Matthew 11:30).

50

Merciful Wisdom

"But the wisdom that comes from heaven is first of all pure; then peace-loving, considerate, submissive,

full of mercy and good fruit...." (James 3:17)

Margaret Mead, the world-renowned anthropologist, was speaking at a university. Following her presentation she hosted a time of questions and dialogue. One student asked her what she considered to be the first sign of civilization in any given culture.

This student, like most in the gathering, was expecting Ms. Mead to talk about fishhooks or clay pots or grinding stones. Her answer surprised them all. She said that the first sign of civilization was represented, in her mind, by a healed femur. The femur is the human thighbone. At the look of uncertain stares, Ms. Mead went on to explain.

Beating the Law of the Jungle

In the law of the jungle, she said, broken femurs never get healed. When a person in the jungle suffers a broken leg, he is left to die. On his own no one ever survives a broken leg long enough to have the bone heal. So, said Ms. Mead, where someone takes the time to protect the one who fell from further attacks, carefully binds up the wound, guards the safety of the one who cannot defend himself, brings food and medicine to the sick, and refuses to let the discouragement of pain lead to suicide, *this* is where civilization starts.

Margaret Mead's picture of the birth of civilization is very powerful picture. It reminds me of the portrait of the "Suffering Servant" that Isaiah paints in chapter 42 of his prophecy. The true Servant of God, says Isaiah, is one who will not break a bruised reed or snuff out a smoldering wick. These weak and damaged things are images of people we know—folks who have been beat up by life; women who have suffered too long at the hands of brutal men; children who starve because the economic and social systems of their lands are cruelly distorted; men who find their hopes dashed in an instant of insane corporate politics.

Enter the Servant of God, says Isaiah. With faithfulness he brings protection and justice. Suddenly the law of the jungle no longer makes sense. As James indicates, this mercy of help and healing is a much higher wisdom.

Pressured by the Jungle

In Ernest Gordon's book *To End All Wars* (Zondervan, 2002) a story that breathes with this divine wisdom is told. It is the true tale of what took place in the Japanese prison-of-war camp made famous by the movie *The Bridge over the River Kwai*. The camp stood at the end of the Bataan death march that brought Allied soldiers deep into the jungles of Asia. Few would survive, and everyone knew it. In order to make the best of a terrible situation they teamed up in pairs, each watching out for a buddy.

One prisoner was a strapping six-foot-three fellow built like a tower of iron. If any could come out of this alive, all felt he would. That was before his buddy got malaria. The smaller fellow was much weaker, and very likely to die. Their captors did not want to deal with sickness, so anyone who was unable to work was confined in a "hot house" until he succumbed to heat exhaustion, dehydration, and the collapse of his bodily systems.

The sick man was locked into a hothouse and left to die. Surprisingly he did not die, because every mealtime his strong buddy went out to him, under curses and threats from the guards, and shared his meager rations. Every night his strong buddy sneaked from the prison barracks, braved the watchful eyes above that held guns of death, and brought his own slim blanket to cover the fevered convulsions of the sick man.

Playing the Game by Different Rules

At the end of two weeks the sick man astounded the guards by recovering well enough to be able to return to work. He even survived the entire camp experience and lived to tell about it. His buddy, however—the strong man all thought invincible—died very shortly of malaria, exposure, and dysentery. He had given his life to save his friend.

The story does not end there. When Allied troops liberated that camp at the close of the war in the Pacific virtually every prisoner was a Christian. There was a symphony orchestra in camp, with instruments made of the crudest materials. There were worship services every Sunday, and the death toll was far lower than any expected. All this because of the silent testimony made by a strong man toward his buddy facing death.

There is much that pretends to be wise in our world, but nothing can match the profound wisdom and strength of true mercy. I wonder how wise I will be today?

51

Impartial Wisdom

"But the wisdom that comes from heaven is first of all pure; then peace-loving, considerate, submissive,
full of mercy and good fruit, impartial...." (James 3:17)

I sat with a man recently whose mother is one of the most impartial people on earth. That does not make her a saint, however. The man wept as he told how his mother had treated each of her children in an equally rotten manner. One after another she had driven them away. They moved to other places just to escape her tirades at their tragic worthlessness. Even now, every time their sense of duty forces them to return to celebrate her birthday or some other holiday, the mother only adds to their guilt by caustically reminding each about how they have all abandoned her.

Weary

I admire the man. On the basis of his Christian faith he has chosen to remain closest to his mother, and to care for her both because she is his mother and because there is no one else left that she has not sadistically prodded away with goads of lacerating venom. The man, in his partiality, is more a saint than his mother, in her impartiality.

In reality that is the key to the wisdom James talks about. The wisdom of heaven, impartial as it is, is based upon the premise that *each* person is special, *each* person is unique, *each* person is worthy of "partial" love.

C. S. Lewis described it well when he said that there are two ways to be impartial in our relationships with others. The first was by reducing each one we meet to the lowest common denominator and disdaining them all equally. In prison, for example, each inmate is the same and thus each is treated "impartially:" names are replaced with numbers; clothing for all is identical; living quarters are reduced to exactly the same size for each person; even the schedule of the day is harmonized until none is given special privileges over another. Impartiality rules.

Worthy

The second way of impartiality, said Lewis, was that of individualized esteem. Here the goal is not to treat each person equally but to treat each person uniquely with a focus on caring. In illustrating his point, Lewis said that he was upset with the way that some of his friends invited their children to call them, as parents, by their first names. While he understood their motives, he feared the outcome.

Their goal in this democratizing of the family was to insure the equality of each person. "If we all call each other by our first names," they said, "we will all be equals." The parents were attempting to teach their children, from early on, that no person truly holds a higher value in society than does anyone else.

Yet, said Lewis, the result of such social conditioning is far worse than its benefit. The beauty of family life is found precisely in the inequalities present. In a family we learn that persons are not to be loved "equally," but "uniquely." A wife does not love her husband because he is just one of the crowd that hangs about. Nor does a father treat one child completely the same as any other child. True love discriminates. Any parent who tries to love all the children in exactly the same way becomes frustrated to the point of incompetence. It is in the family that we learn to esteem each person greatly *not* because each is another cloned pea in a pod, but because each is unique and different.

Wise

In this lies the secret of impartial wisdom. A person who cares with an impartial love does not look at all persons the same. Rather, a person who cares impartially begins with the assumption that each person is different, and each person is worthy of individual love.

When my grandmother died, testimonies poured in from everywhere: "She was a great woman!" "We always respected her!" "She never played favorites!" "She always cared about me!" My grandmother was a wise woman. She didn't treat every person in exactly the same way. She treated each person in a special way. It was the grace of her "partial" attitude toward each that made her exceptionally impartial.

52

Sincere Wisdom

"But the wisdom that comes from heaven is first of all pure; then peace-loving, considerate, submissive, full of mercy and good fruit, impartial and sincere." (James 3:17)

At the time of the French Revolution a group of university students observed the French Assembly in its attempt to create a new code of law for the unfolding age of the Republic. They were appalled at the long-winded speeches and pompous debates that seemed more geared to personal pride than to the public good.

When they voiced their harsh opinions to the honorable Gabriel Mirabeau, champion of the Revolution, he gave them some interesting advice. "Laws," he said, "are like sausages. You should never watch them being made."

Purity

Mirabeau was a man of other insights as well. When he first heard a passionate public speech by fellow Revolutionary statesman Robespierre, he said, "This man will go far; he believes what he says!"

That truth wasn't lost on the crowds. They used to say of Robespierre that he was an "incorruptible" man. He was the same man on the street as he was in the privacy of drawing rooms where the devious games of politics were played. Whether Robespierre had the best view of society for the good of the people in France's changing times will always be debated. But his heart was never questioned.

To believe what you say, and to say what you believe is the soul of sincerity. The Bible calls it purity of heart, where motives are unmixed. What you see is what you get. Religiously, there is great value in sincerity. "Blessed are the pure in heart," said Jesus, "for they will see God."

Patience

Purity of heart coupled with patience is a strong virtue. When Groen van Prinsterer waged his lonely battle in the Dutch House of Commons for a biblically shaped world of justice, it was his sincerity of faith that carried him along. In fact, when Abraham Kuyper met van Prinsterer on the evening of May 18, 1869, in one of the rooms of the great church in Utrecht, the strength of van Prinsterer's convictions coupled with his patient plodding toward the utopia of the vision of God's great Kingdom so inspired Kuyper that it became the driving force of his own political career.

More than twenty-five years later Kuyper said that when he met van Prinsterer that night, he became a "spiritual son" to the man. No one who held to his convictions with such patience, said Kuyper, could be far from the truth.

Passion

Patient purity of faith is a powerful inner strength. Combine it with passion, and it becomes a quality of leadership. Canada's Joe Clark always displayed purity of convictions and patience in politics, yet he never exuded the passion that evoked national allegiance. The same was true of Jimmy Carter in the United States. No one doubted the sincerity of his faith or the tenacity of his willingness to carry through on policy, but passion was not Carter's forte.

Passion is a slippery thing. If it rises without inner substance it can destroy others with violence, or else carry them along in the hollowness of mere entertainment. An American once complained to marshal Ferdinand Foch, commander of the French military at the start of World War I, that the politeness

167

of French conversations seemed insincere. "There is nothing in it," he said, "but wind."

Foch replied, "There is nothing but wind in a tire, but it makes riding in a car very smooth and pleasant."

Maybe so. But there are times in life when we need more than wind, more than T. S. Eliot's "hollow men" who are distracted by distractions. Passion that flows from purity of heart in a life given to patient plodding toward the Kingdom of God has great power.

Follow the person with that kind of wisdom!

53

Back to the Farm

"Peacemakers who sow in peace raise a harvest of righteousness." (James 3:18)

The other day as I bit into my sandwich at lunch I realized just how far I had strayed from the farm of my youth. My sandwich had alfalfa sprouts on it! Can you imagine that? When I was growing up alfalfa was for cattle, not people! How life changes!

Learning the Basics

Baling alfalfa was about the worst summer job on the farm. It always happened during the sultry heat of June and July. The dust filled our noses and lungs, and getting those bales stacked up in the hayloft of our old barn was about like handling cacti in a sauna where the air was 50% dust. We wore out pairs of gloves and blue jeans every day, and scratched our arms and legs and chest raw. It may have been on one of those hot afternoons that I contemplated *not* taking over the family farm.

Farmers have their own set of jokes. A few years back the Quay County Sun newspaper in Tucumcari, New Mexico, carried this ad: **"Farmer with 160 irrigated acres wants marriage-minded woman with tractor. When replying, please show picture of the tractor."** (AP release, June 1978).

Or take the story of Victor Borge, the famous pianist. When he decided to buy a chicken farm a friend asked him, "Do you know anything about breeding chickens?"

"No," said Borge, "but the chickens do!"

Living the Battle

One of my favorite farming tales is of a pastor in a rural congregation who was tired of hearing people complain about their lot in life. Every year the stories changed, but they always had the same theme: farming is tough. It is tough because you cannot count on the weather. Or the bugs are sure to get your crop. And the cost of seed and fertilizer is always too high, while the price of grain is way too low. Besides, the spring was too wet; we couldn't get into the fields on time. And, wouldn't you know it? Frost came too early in September; the corn didn't ripen properly.

One year, though, everything happened just right. The spring was beautiful. The fields were in perfect condition. The rains fell at exactly the right times. The harvest was the largest ever, and the market prices were excellent.

So the pastor said to one farmer, who always found something black in every bright spot, "Well, that was some year, wasn't it? Nothing to complain about *this* time!"

The man didn't miss a heartbeat. He just looked that pastor straight in the eye and said, "Reverend, it's a year like this that really makes the soil tired!"

Looking for the Blessing

Farming is rarely easy, no matter what one grows. Certainly, in our world, peace is a difficult crop to raise. Beside the "wars and rumors of wars" that Jesus promised would cling like taxes to every society, there is the nasty tension of competitive egos on the wrestling mat of work and the inner turmoil of changing identities that compete for dominance.

Peace comes in a variety of shapes and sizes, when we do experience its brief illumination. A quiet walk along the beach at sunset. Morning mists hanging in secluded pockets of a July cornfield. The methodic metronome of a grandfather clock next to a glowing tree, timing the magical minutes until Christmas morning.

Peace can be the first song of a bird following a barrage of artillery fire in Kosovo. Or it can creep in like the first rays of sunlight breaking through the hurricane at sea.

But the peace that James envisions is noisy. It is the sweaty grunt of psychological and spiritual combat. It involves the struggles for justice between warring nations as well as the tedious arbitration of a counselor fighting with hissing spouses to save a marriage. The peace of God is one that cost the price of blood.

Those who sow its drops in the torment of these times may never see the harvest until the soils of earth grow too tired to raise another crop. Fortunately, God has planned a second season for the Tree of Life to flourish. Then the waters of justice will flow in the garden of righteousness, and the weekly "Peacemakers" conferences will erupt into a perennial convention.

54

The Cancer of Consumerism

"What causes fights and quarrels among you? Don't they come from your desires that battle within you?
You want something but don't get it. You kill and covet, but you cannot have what you want. You quarrel
and fight. You do not have, because you do not ask God. When you ask, you do not receive, because you
ask with wrong motives, that you may spend what you get on your pleasures." (James 4:1-3)

I know a mother who remembers an embarrassing moment that happened when she went with her daughter's class on a school field trip. When the mother showed up with her car, the daughter hid at the back of the group as it was gathering. One more vehicle was needed to transport all of the students, so my friend offered to drive. At first her daughter didn't want to ride with this mother, and tried to get into one of the vans. When she was taken by the hand and led to join her mother, the girl slouched in the back seat and never said a word for the rest of the day.

Was she embarrassed by her mother? No. It was the car. The family car was ten years old and had begun to show some rust.

Hunger

When this woman told me the story she shook her head with some disappointment. She was mildly upset with her daughter who showed such fickleness, but she was more distraught with a society that would teach her children that worth was tied to shiny cars and expensive clothes.

Theirs was not a poor family. They could afford to buy a newer car. Yet the old car ran well. They had talked about it and decided that even though they could afford something more expensive, they would not take the step.

I admire that family. We live in a grossly consumer-driven world. Our society shouts that if we want something we *deserve* to get it. We *need* to buy it. Paying on credit is our *responsibility* to keep the wheels of consumerism turning and the wealth of the nations flowing.

When a person is addicted to drugs he can't stop. He needs the next fix, the next hit, the next pill. When alcoholism grips, a woman will do anything to get another bottle. But what about the addictions of the soul that society says are okay? What about the fads of fashion and culture that rule our shopping habits, and our eating habits, and our sexual habits?

Healing

Do I wear garments less expensive than I can afford? Can I drive a car less costly than I have the means to buy? Am I able to develop a relationship with someone else without jumping into bed before marriage? Do I have the strength of character to go against the grain?

Often we don't know until we have tested our souls in the x-rays of deliberate abstinence. G. K. Chesterton put it this way. "Art and morality have this in common," he said. "They both know where to draw the lines."

When we know where to draw the lines on a picture, it begins to have beauty and meaning. When we know where to draw the lines on a building, it begins to have shape and purpose. And when we know where to draw the lines in our lives, we begin to have character. The person who will stop at nothing will say yes to anything. The man who has no limits also has no identity of his own. He robs it from the victims of his cruelties. The woman who doesn't know how to say no will never be able to say yes to the things in life that matter most. Even the child who isn't taught the boundaries of behavior grows up to be an adult without a conscience.

Hope

Some years ago *People* magazine interviewed Dolly Parton. At one point the reporter asked, "Where do you ever get such a strong character?"

Dolly replied that it came from her Christian faith. "I quote the Bible real good," said Dolly.

"What about psychiatry?" asked the interviewer. "So many people find the need to get counseling, especially in the stressed of show business."

"No," said Dolly, "I don't see a psychiatrist. I fast instead."

"You what?"

"I fast."

"Is that like a diet?"

"No," said Dolly. "I do it to get in touch with God. Sometimes I'll... fast 7, 14, or 21 days. I don't drink nothing but water and I don't ever say when I'm on a fast --- Scripture says you're not supposed to" (*People*, January 19, 1981). She went on to say that she never made a major decision without fasting and prayer. The interviewer was astounded.

I don't think James would be. He would probably thank God for some sanity still present in the rotting stink of a society gripped by the cancer of covetousness.

55

A Marriage Made in Heaven

"You adulterous people, don't you know that friendship with the world is hatred toward God? Anyone who chooses to be a friend of the world becomes and enemy of God." (James 4:4)

A woman was working in her flower garden under the intense scrutiny of her 4-year-old neighbor. As they got into a conversation, the young girl suddenly gave out this startling revelation: "When I grow up I'm going to marry Danny." Danny was a 6-year-old boy living in the house just down the street.

The woman was curious. "Why are you going to marry Danny?" she asked.

"I have to," said the little one. "I'm not allowed to cross the street to where the other boys live."

Wedding

She makes marriage sound so simple! Locate the closest partner, and then just stick together!

It is not like that though, is it? *Finding* the right partner is work enough for most of us. *Staying* together is a much bigger deal. Allison and Gary (not their real names) were just one of the couples that showed the stress of marriage in my attempts, over the years, to help people stick together.

They were high school sweethearts and obviously in love when they first came to talk with me about marriage. Their backgrounds were similar and they had dated for over five years, so they knew each other well.

We spent six sessions together in marriage preparation, talking, among other things, about the "Big 3:" money, communication, and time commitments. They seemed to have a good handle on how their relationship would unfold.

The wedding was beautiful. It came off with only one slight hitch—the photographer was absolutely certain that she should capture every important moment, so when her camera ran out of film just as the two were reciting their vows, she came up to the front and intruded, asking them to stop until she could change the roll! At that point they were flustered enough and I was dumbfounded enough to stop the action. I never let that happen again during a wedding ceremony!

Still the celebration was magnificent. Both families agreed together that Allison and Gary were off to a great start.

Marriage

Three years later Allison and Gary made an appointment with me. Things were a bit rocky in their marriage. Both were faithful to each other, yet each had begun to resent the time the other was spending on outside interests. Gary was into cars and racing; Allison delighted in clothes and work and friends.

There was a bristling of the air when they talked. Something wasn't right, and they knew it. Allison's mom wanted them to talk with me, since she knew that marriage was for life. The two of them were not as convinced about the permanence of marriage, and both hinted that they might be ready to pack it in.

A year later they were separated. The house was sold. Gary took an apartment and Allison moved back in with her parents. The next year they got a divorce.

Commitment

What happened?

When I talked with Allison about it all, she said something very interesting. She said she always felt as if they were each listening to different music. Gary had the rumbling beat and twang of Country in him, and she moved to the provocative drive of Rhythm & Blues. It was not that they particularly liked those two styles of music; rather, said Allison, it was a sense that each of them was responding to a different note or melody or beat in life. They couldn't get it together.

Eventually both Allison and Gary moved in with other people. Neither married again. Their one attempt at finding "the right one" had convinced them that it would never happen again.

It wouldn't take very much to change the names and tell the story of Christians who "left their first love" with Jesus. Marriage is a lot like Christianity, and Christianity a lot like marriage, just as Paul put it in Ephesians 5.

Some marriages go down in a blaze of adultery. So do some testimonies of Christian faith. Most, however, slip away through failed friendships. The bursts of passionate love and emotional testimony slide away as people forget to *live* together. George Santayana put it this way: "He liked to walk alone; she liked to walk alone. So they got married and walked alone together." In the end, that is a recipe for disaster.

We all need to choose our friends wisely. If we want our marriages to last, we need the glue of friendship to make it happen. So, says James, in our religion. Don't flirt with too many "best friends" in this world if you want to stay out of divorce court on Judgment Day.

56

Choosing Our Enemies

"Anyone who chooses to be a friend of the world becomes an enemy of God. Or do you think Scripture

says without reason that the spirit he caused to live in us envies intensely?" (James 4:4-5)

Every good story is told best through the rim of darkness and shadow. I think of the conflict between the composers Wolfgang Amadeus Mozart and Antonio Salieri in 18th century Vienna. Salieri was the official "court musician," and he had a right to be. He worked hard at his craft, writing hummable melodies and decent choral pieces.

Envy

Salieri was a devout Christian, and had prayed passionately for God to bless him in his musical efforts. His appointment in the royal precincts seemed to confirm God's gracious response.

Then came Mozart. He was a boy wonder, a child prodigy. He would dazzle the crowds, playing at music like it was as natural as the air he breathed, and as trivial a thing as some simple toy. Mozart's fingers danced at the keyboard, and his melodies for instruments and choirs were both complex and fun at the same time. When he directed the orchestra it seemed as if heaven came alive on earth through Mozart's soaring songs.

Salieri was green with envy. More than that, he was bitter at the unfairness of it all. To put it bluntly, Mozart was as obvious a sinner as Salieri was a saint! Mozart was immature, vulgar and obscene. He made off with the ladies of the court and the street time and again.

Desire

Salieri was incensed. Why should God shower such talents on Mozart while he, Salieri, worked his devotion to music with incredible drudgery? Why should Mozart traffic only in worldly pleasures, and still succeed so divinely?

When Mozart died from some mysteriously induced poisoning, Salieri's eyes gleamed vengefully. Yet Mozart's demise never restored to Salieri the esteem he coveted among the Viennese elite. He ended his days in an insane asylum, cursing God for denying him the kind talent that Mozart had displayed with a profane playfulness.

Desire and envy are twin sisters within us. Our thirst for God and his goodness rises from the same heart that can jealously seek fame and fortune over the heads of rivals. If you have ever been hurt in life, if you have ever been passed over for a promotion, if you have ever been struck down by a disease or a disability you didn't count on, if you have ever watched others sail right on through waters that swamped your boat, or soar on winds that plastered your craft against the cliff, you know what Salieri tasted whenever crowds applauded Mozart.

Grace

We choose our enemies more quickly than we choose our friends. Wise is the person who knows enough about the character of God to choose for enemies those powers that set themselves over against grace. If we don't choose our enemies carefully, we may end up failing to be friends of God.

57

Grace

"But he gives us more grace." (James 4:6)

Anne Sexton wrote a volume of poetry describing her religious journey as *The Awful Rowing Toward God*. Faith is difficult, she said in her poems, not so much because God wants it to be that way, but because other elements including our own hearts conspire against us on the way.

Twisting the Game

In her concluding poem, "The Rowing Endeth," Anne pictured herself docking her spiritual boat at the island of God's home. There she sat down to play poker with God, attempting to win access to God's wealth. In the heat of the game she knew she held a winning hand, laying down a straight royal flush! Even God couldn't beat that!

But God only smiled and spread down a hand of *five* aces! The joke was on Anne, and they laughed together in great gusto, echoing grace to the corners of heaven.

It was a strange parable that Anne Sexton penned, yet one rich with biblical meaning. We are forever playing games with God, trying to win his chips and bankroll his mercy. Still, sly and wily as we might be, God always manages to pull out a trump card we never expected. Sometimes it even seems like he isn't playing by the rules (our rules, of course!). Yet when he shows his hand, and takes the game, it is only to share the winnings with us in lavish ways we didn't deserve.

Talking of Grace

Anne's picture is a delightful portrait of grace. Grace, as many have written, is very difficult to define. Frederick Buechner said that most tears are grace, as is the smell of rain and having somebody love you. Lewis Smedes said that grace is amazing because it works against our common sense. Inside we know that we are too weak, too harassed, and too human to change for the better, and life shouts that we are caught in a rut of fate or futility; yet God somehow gives us a tomorrow better than we could have chosen for ourselves, were we to have the strength to make it happen. That's grace.

A friend of mine knows it too well. Today she took me out to lunch, and spilled another tale of woe. Life has been very unkind to her. Few of us could survive with the hand she has been dealt. Even when she tries to play with the cards she has, the numbers on them keep changing, and she has to start all over learning the game.

Tiptoeing toward Glory

Three things have made it possible for her to keep going: friends who cared enough to look past her quirks and craziness, medications that kept her from winding up a bag-lady on the streets, and grace. At every corner in her life, just as the traffic was threatening her from both directions, God met her. God took her hand. God played a trump card and she had safe passage to the next corner.

Call it chance, if you will. Call it luck. Maybe it was all in the cards.

But then, with Anne Sexton, I believe in the One who dealt them. And, with James, in the One who holds five aces when needed.

58

Enemy of the Proud

"That is why Scripture says: 'God opposes the proud but gives grace to the humble.'" (James 4:6)

Do you remember Rudyard Kipling's tale of "How the Camel Got Its Hump"? At the dawn of creation, according to Kipling, God gave each of his wonderful animals a job to do. Working together they began to prepare the new world for the coming of humankind.

The only one among them that would not work was the camel. Whenever the other animals asked for his help, he just said, "Humph!!" and walked away. The camel, according to Kipling, thought he was better than all the other animals, so he "Humph!!"ed around every day with his proud nose in the air, and a disdainful swagger in his legs.

But when God saw what was happening, he collected all of the haughty camel's "Humph!!"s, and one day dumped them right down onto the camel's back. And that, said Kipling, is how the camel got its hump.

One Step Too High

Proud people a lot like camels, aren't they? Noses in the air, swaggering steps, and humps of self-importance pushing up wherever they invade the company of others. Mid-20th century Italian dictator Benito Mussolini played the part so well. Although he was short of stature he was long on pride. People used to say that he could strut even when he was sitting down. A newspaper once reported that "He was a solemn procession of one."

Pride is a funny thing. It is an extension of many very good qualities that God has given us as gifts. Why, then, does a great athlete cross the line from confidence to cockiness? What pushes a beautiful woman from graciousness to arrogance? When does a businessman step up one rung too high on the ladder of success and become self-important?

The ancient Greeks tried to define the transition from piety to pride in the story of Narcissus. Narcissus was a wonderfully beautiful young man, greatly talented and admired. Unfortunately he had ears large enough to hear the whispers of appreciation that buzzed through every crowd when he approached. Soon he began to believe what others said, and then fell in love with himself.

Falling in Love with Ourselves

One the day he was scrambling through the rocks of the hills on a hunt. Thirsty, he paused at a pool in the hollows, and bent down to drink. But before his lips broke the mirrored surface he caught sight of a marvelous water nymph staring at him from below. He was entranced by the beautiful face, the wonderful eyes, the marvelous nose and chin, and reached down to embrace the nymph.

Yet when he disturbed the water it seemed as if the nymph scurried away. That pained him deeply and he began to cry. But when the ripples subsided, the nymph was back. Though Narcissus didn't seem to catch on, he was actually seeing himself.

Over and over the scene repeated itself—Narcissus staring in love at his own reflection in the pool—until he finally fell famished to his death!

The point was clear: the moment we begin to love ourselves as the highest good we lose the power to live authentically. We cross the line from piety to pride when we become the object of our own appreciation.

Beyond Obsession

This is a perplexing issue, however, since we all need self-esteem to function to our fullest potential. The concern in the Bible becomes a matter of where that self-esteem originates. When we are loved by another, our self-esteem grows. The source of the power is located outside of ourselves and energizes us to be the best we can be. Once we fall in love with ourselves, the empowerment becomes cancerous, and we destroy the very qualities that might otherwise make us lovely.

Tony Campolo said it well. When he was in seminary, taking his first class in preaching, he was already a very gifted speaker. After his first "practice" sermon to his fellow-students and professor, his peers praised him up one side and down the other. He couldn't wait to see what his professor wrote.

The evaluation came back with a single line in red marking ink: "Tony, you can't convince people that you're wonderful and that Jesus is wonderful in the same sermon."

That is why James says that God opposes the proud. I cannot love anyone else when I am obsessed with myself, even if my obsession is for holy living or righteous behavior.

59

Submission

"Submit yourselves, then, to God." (James 4:7)

Friends in Alberta used to tell of an uncle who married late in life. His bride was a feisty widow who sparkled with energy. The wedding took place on a farm in the old family home.

At the appropriate moment in the ceremony the pastor asked the bride, "Do you promise to love, honor, and obey him?"

She hesitated, face scrunched in thought. "Love and honor—yes," she finally responded. "Obey—no!"

Both the pastor and the groom were taken aback. What to do now?

It was the groom who broke the impasse. "Two out of three isn't bad," he said, and the wedding went on.

Saving Face

Obedience and submission are scarce commodities in most of our lives. There are probably at least two reasons for that. For one thing, we are self-made people. Early in life we make it clear that "I do it *myself*!" We have a need to be right, a need to save face. One of my friends has a cartoon on his office door that pictures a senior official standing grimly in front of a subordinate's desk. The boss says, "I didn't say it was your fault; I said I was going to blame you."

There is a lot of that in all of our lives. Since Adam and Eve passed the blame along to others we all try to outwit reality in order to save face. We need to be right. We need to be strong. We need to be identified as "winners" rather than "losers." Submission is for the weaklings, not the strong.

Saving Space

A second reason why we hesitate to submit to anyone else is that we don't know if we can trust the other person. One man in his middle years can recount to me every promise his father made to him and then broke, when he was a lad. To this day he finds it hard to trust God. After all, as a wise person has noted, "'Daddy' is the name for God on the lips of a child." When parents fail us (and they always will), we learn mistrust in the religious core of our beings. In order to keep from getting hurt we won't submit, even to God.

Wise pastors have always known that. Yet they continue to encourage people to trust and submit because it is the essence of who we are as humans in our relationship to the Creator of the universe.

In the early church a teaching tale told of a young girl lived with her parents in a cottage at the edge of a dense forest. "Don't wander too far into the woods," they told her. "You might get lost."

A warm summer's day with birds singing and winds calling, however, carried the girl's feet deeper and deeper into the cool underbrush. The shadows were long before she realized how lost she was. Yelling and crying, she dashed one way and the next, not finding home and working herself into convulsions of panic.

Meanwhile, her parents were worried as well. In the dusk of evening they called her name and made forays into the woods. As thoughts of all the worst fates attacked them, they organized villagers and other neighbors into search parties.

By dawn the young girl was sleeping exhausted on a bed of pine needles, and only her father was left of the many searchers. As he stumbled into the clearing and saw her, his footsteps broke branches and sent birds twittering. The noise awoke her and she saw him. Jumping to her feet she ran toward him, arms outstretched. "Daddy! Daddy!" she cried. "I found you!"

Saving Grace

So it is in our lives. When we finally find God, "on our own," as we might say, it is a moment of great excitement for us. Yet when the whole story is told us again, in our later years, we realize just how patient and persistent has been God's own search for us.

At that point we no longer need to put on religious airs. Then, too, submission sounds like a natural thing.

60

Resist

"Resist the devil, and he will flee from you." (James 4:7)

A newly married couple moved into their first apartment. Marketing experts immediately targeted them, and salesmen for everything from laundry service to life insurance besieged them. While they were still busy unpacking a dairyman came to the door. The young bride tried to turn him away. "My husband and I don't drink milk," she said.

"I'd be glad to deliver a quart every morning for cooking," he persisted.

"That's more than I need," she replied curtly, and began to close the door.

"Well, ma'am, how about some cream? Strawberries are just coming in at the market, and..."

"No!" she insisted. "We never use cream."

The man backed away slowly and the wife congratulated herself on her sales resistance. The truth of the matter was that they had already ordered from another dairy and she just wanted to get rid of the fellow.

The following morning, however, the same dairyman appeared at the door with a bowl of plump, ripe strawberries in one hand and a half-pint bottle of cream in the other. "Lady," he said as he poured the cream over the berries and handed them to her, "I got to thinking---you sure have missed a lot!" They had a laugh, she got the breakfast treat of her life, and he got a weekly order for milk!

Gravity and Grace

Persistence often conquers resistance, especially when it carries a bowl of fresh strawberries in one hand. While often the pleasure gained is harmless, there are times when it is deadly. Following the path of least resistance, as one person put it, is what makes people and rivers crooked. "A bargain," said another, "is something you cannot use at a price you cannot resist." That is why Martin Luther cautioned his followers, telling them that there were three conversions necessary to gain eternal life: of the heart, the mind, and the wallet. "The latter," said Luther, "is the most resistant."

We need to learn resistance in many ways in order to survive in life. When two Russian cosmonauts returned to earth in 1982 after 211 days in space they suffered from dizziness, high pulse rates and heart palpitations. They couldn't walk for a week. A month later they were still undergoing therapy for atrophied muscles and weakened hearts. In the zero gravity of outer space their muscles had begun to waste away. Scientists had to design "resistance suits" to counteract the unseen predator. Only with resistance applied against the muscles of the body could they remain strong.

Ben Weir, in his book *Hostage Bound, Hostage Free* (Westminster, 1987) translates this into spiritual terms. He documents the inner resistance that saved his life. During his many months of captivity in Beirut there was a constant nagging to give in to depression and give up to despair. Although his situation was excessive, far beyond that which we normally face, it condensed into 18 months the wasting that can happen in any spirit over the years. Charles Darwin, who grew up in a strong Presbyterian home, said, in his later years, that he never rejected the Christian faith; instead, he said, it gradually lost its importance to him as he ceased to use it. No resistance, no resurgence. No test, no tensile. No effort, no energy.

Growth

Someone told me recently of a young man who was buying his own clothes in preparation for college. He asked a sales clerk what the tag meant when it said "Shrink Resistant." The clerk replied, "Even though that shirt doesn't want to shrink, it will!"

Most of us could wear a label like that on our souls. Only the disciplines of faith cause it to fall off as our resistance to the devil grows.

61

Approach

"Come near to God and he will come near to you." (James 4:8)

When our oldest daughter began driver's training she needed to spend 50 hours behind the wheel of our car with either Brenda or myself riding next to her. She was supposed to be practicing the fine art of motoring, while we were mandated by the state of Michigan to teach her the best of our skills.

A New Perspective

I'm not used to sitting in the front passenger seat. I like to drive, and when we are in the car together as family my foot naturally searches for the accelerator. From my new perch on the other side of the car, however, I can spend more time observing the driving habits of others.

Intersections with four-way stops prove especially interesting. Some drivers plow right through, hardly caressing the brake pedal. They know that they have right-of-way whether the law gives it or not. One car I saw recently even sported this bumper sticker: **"AS A MATTER OF FACT, I DO OWN THE ROAD!"** That driver knew that stop signs were posted in order to keep other people out of his way!

Other drivers are much more hesitant at those all-way stop intersections. They halt their vehicles far short of the stop signs, and then gradually play off the others who might have cars pointed in different directions. Stop! Start! Stop! Start! Stop! Roll forward! Stop! After a while no one is quite sure who should pass through next.

Check It Out

A few drivers are very legalistic. When they arrive at intersections at the same time with other vehicles they assess, in inches, which car got there first. They will wave on that driver, even if others are beginning to make false starts. Not only that, but where two or more cars pulled up at the same time, these drivers live by the rule that the driver on the right goes first. They will not move until it is their turn.

Some (fortunately not very many) seem to find driving a nuisance or an opportunity to do the things they really prefer: talking, finding the right music on the radio, dressing, shaving, or changing cigarettes. A week ago I followed a woman who had mastered the art of styling her hair while driving. For two city block she managed to apply hairspray while driving with her knees!

Sometimes in my musing about drivers I consider matching their personalities with their motoring habits. Is the timid driver a low "D" on the **DiSC** scale, or an "I"ntrovert with Myers-Briggs? Does the legalist need to accomplish her **DiSC** "C"ompliance skills in order to have her day begin and end perfectly? Are those who nose ahead into intersections merely acting on their high "D"ominance characteristics, or are they simply extreme "E"xtroverts, as Kiersey and Bates would have it?

Trafficking in Prayer

Of course, with my pastoring and theological bent, I often wonder whether people pray like they drive. "Come near to God," says James. I can see one driver I know racing for heaven, scattering angels on the way to the throne. Another peeps sheepishly from around an ecclesiastical corner, wondering if this is really the place she ought to be. A third person I have traveled with marks his prayers, as his life, with logical precision and careful diction, giving God the time and date in the same manner he signals turns to others on earthly thoroughfares.

I think of my own driving, and my own approach to God. Sometimes I think I must make him just one more stop along the busy highway of life, hoping that the prayer ramps will be easy-off, easy-on while I rush through doing my thing with him.

It takes all kinds, I guess. What I am learning these days, however, is that is always wonderful to hear the car come home, no matter how skilled, aggressive or hesitant the driver. That is why I always try to greet my daughter when she pulls in. After playing with life on the roads, it *is* good to see her.

I can imagine, as James says, that God is always happy when we come home to him as well, no matter how or where we drive our souls.

62

Hand Washing

"Wash your hands, you sinners, and purify your hearts, you double-minded." (James 4:8)

We stopped at a fast-food restaurant one day for a quick bite between shopping excursions. The food preparation area was open to the serving counter and with a rush of patrons we stood watching workers create burritos and tacos. One teen on staff was obviously struggling with a cold or perhaps even a more severe virus. He walked past us several times, sneezing twice into his open hand. Then he went to a back wall, passed his hands under a dispenser but avoided the sink, turned to the food preparation counter, and began to toss together the ingredients for our order. His nose was running, and every 15-20 seconds he would sniff loudly.

The woman next to me, also waiting for her food, said, "He didn't wash his hands!" The man on the other side of her shook his head in disgust. I said to the person at the counter, whose nametag carried the designation **ASSISTANT MANAGER**, "Excuse me, but that young man didn't wash his hands before working with the food. He was just sneezing, and he didn't wash his hands!"

The young man heard our conversations. He walked up to the counter with a belligerent look and said, "I did too wash my hands!"

"No you didn't!" said the woman next to me. "I saw everything you did, and you didn't wash your hands!"

"I saw the same thing," I said.

He was angry now. "Here!" he said, shoving his hands up to my nose. "You want to smell?"

By now I was disgusted, my appetite was gone, and our daughters were thoroughly embarrassed by the fuss. I backed away, he finished preparing our food, we nibbled at some of it, threw most of it away, and left quickly. We have never gone back there to eat. We're not finicky about most things, but that episode of unwashed hands left us shivering with distaste.

Touchy-Feely Trauma

Most of us have tried to get away without washing our hands at one time or another. When our mothers called us to the meal table we were often too hungry to wash, or couldn't be bothered. Whatever germs we devoured from dirty hands became our own menace, and usually no one else's.

But when another person's carelessness spreads threats of the plague in a public arena we become concerned. No one wants a doctor to perform open-heart surgery without scrubbing up first. No one wants to shake hands with a careless trash hauler. No parent wants a childcare attendant to change the baby's diaper and feed that child without a ritual cleansing in between.

Stop the Plague

When we were living in Nigeria a plague of pinkeye swept through the region. Nearly every one of my students suffered from it—tearing, sore eyes, sniffles. Most people in the market place at Gboko displayed symptoms. The doctor at our mission station warned us: "Wash your hands as often as possible, and don't touch your eyes."

So we washed. And we tried to keep our hands from our eyes. Amazingly, we never got pinkeye in our family.

That was a good lesson in the value of hand washing. Sometimes we need to get rid of the dirt that clings when we work. Sometimes we are preparing ourselves for something special, like a date or a banquet. Sometimes, with Pilate at the trial of Jesus, we are showing symbolically that we want to be rid of a matter that irritates us. And sometimes, as our doctor reminded us, we are trying to prevent the spread of disease.

Deep Cleansing

Shakespeare wrote a scene that can also take hand washing one level deeper. When Lady McBeth conspires with her husband to murder Duncan, the righteous indignation of divine morality vexes her mind until the stains of Duncan's blood seem indelibly imprinted on her palms. She roams sleeplessly, rubbing her hands raw in a futile attempt to cleanse them, muttering, "Out, damned spot!"

Some stains, however, run too deep for water. Only the soap of grace can change the hue of human flesh and keep the plague of sin from passing along from one victim to the next.

63

Restless Realism

"Grieve, mourn and wail. Change your laughter to mourning and your joy to gloom." (James 4:9)

It was a funeral I didn't expect with a family I didn't know, the aftermath of a tragedy I couldn't comprehend. Two men drinking at a party, the younger man dating the older man's daughter. A friendly scuffle? Or was it pent-up resentment that never before spied from the shadows? A gun. A mock "shooting match." Scared friends and family. Another shot in the barn out back. A smoking weapon in the older man's hand; the younger man dead on the ground.

Woeful Weavings

Someone in our congregation took his friend from work to our worship services. For three months he and his common-law wife and children came on Sunday morning. He told me that he needed God. He told me that he found God at our church. He told me that his life was changing.

Now he sat steaming in my office. It was his brother that was murdered last night, and he wanted to kill the murderer! First things first, however. I was the only "priest" he knew. Could I officiate at the funeral?

The spattered blood of death became the spattered ink of chatter in our community, gossiped out of every media newsstand. The shooter was a white male, part of a prominent "old" family in our area, a black sheep lingering at the scandalous end of former glory. The dead man swaggered in on another, newer ethnic wave. Hidden behind his charismatic charm was a long record of drugs, theft, drunkenness and sexual promiscuity.

Mixed Mourning

Of course, the plot thickened. The man with the gun turned out to be brother-in-law to one of my best friends, a member of our congregation and someone I met with monthly in an accountability group. Their stories differed from that of the young brother who asked me to speak at the funeral. My friend and his family emptied their life savings into a fund to buy the best legal counsel for their obviously innocent relative. The angry brother, new Christian and newcomer to our worship services, didn't know the unspoken protocol of "assigned seating" in our worship space, and sat right in front of the woman whose brother shot his brother. Now the newcomer worshipped with great urgency of heart, while the couple behind him and his common-law family fumed worshiplessly.

The funeral was horribly difficult. I knew too much and not enough. Where is God in all of this?

Cleansing Compassion

When we gathered around the casket in the cemetery I spoke a few words of committal, offered prayer, and then encouraged the brother to speak. He wept. He moved from shoulder to shoulder, shuddering grief on every neck. As the casket was lowered into the earth he jumped down on it and blanketed it spread-eagle with his body. He wailed a litany of loss and sorrow and vengeance that pummeled away any other sound. The world grew chill and still.

Weep, children, for the loss of innocence in this world!

Weep, brothers, for the cruelty of life!

Weep, mothers, for the children who die before their times!

Weep, fathers, for the pain that shatters polite society!

Weep, sisters, for the complex soap opera sponsored by life itself!

Weep, people of God, for a world gone mad, for a creation sucked into its own black hole, for the night of evil and the day of gray.

Weep for the reign of Death that lingers too long. Weep until the whisper of Easter shatters these heavy chains and restless souls begin again to hum the doxology.

"Jesus wept." *(John 11:35)*

64

Up the Down Stairs

"Humble yourselves before the Lord, and he will lift you up." (James 4:10)

Yesterday I watched several children playing in the childcare room of our church. One young girl was attempting to slide down a very small slide at the side of an exercise apparatus. To her chagrin a boy half her size was determined to run up the slide first, and obnoxiously pushed his tiny weight at her, leaving her stunned and helpless.

Riding against the Rhythm

It reminded me of the first time my sisters and I saw escalators at the Minneapolis-St. Paul airport. One of my younger sisters stepped gingerly on the "up" escalator, only to change her frightened mind as the machine swept her away. By now she was flowing upward faster than she could march down the unforgiving steps. Not only that, but those who stepped onto the escalator after her blocked the path of her longed-for descent, trapping her on a wailing ride to "Departures."

Once we learned the system, however, we began to play up and down games on the crossing escalators. If the way was clear the fastest among us could chase the "down" stairs up to the top, and leap our way down the "up" escalators to "Arrivals."

Of course, it is very hard to go against the flow. Our own children played the same games when they were younger, and we, as dutiful parents, admonished them appropriately. Yet there are still times when (secretly) I want to try again to "beat the escalator" and prove that even this mechanical apparatus cannot dictate its will over mine.

The Will and the Woe

Part of that desire comes from my strong-willed disposition. There are times when any challenge in life will energize my will and give me the determination to beat the odds. I once wrestled a pig in pen of mud at a Canada Day town celebration just because someone said that I, as a young minister, would never do something like that!

A strong will is a funny thing. Dr. James Dobson earned a small fortune from his book *The Strong-Willed Child*, advising parents how to break the will without hurting the psyche in their children. At the same time, one of our local successful companies refused to hire a friend of mine (a hard-working genius) because he wasn't "gutsy" enough. The implication was that he didn't have a strong enough will to see a business challenge through to a financially beneficial end.

In faith, too, our wills play a larger part than we often suppose. Some people stubbornly believe in trite codes of ethics that they claim to be religious faith, while others meander about holding the sails of their souls to the wind of the latest fads without regard for moral principles. One stubborn "religious" woman told me to my face that she and her family had gotten rid of other pastors and church staff in the past and they would do the same to our choir director. Another young man bounces from congregation to congregation, and, more recently, from religious faith to religious faith, on the whim of the times and the excitement or the promises of the best religious offers.

Descending into Greatness

Jesus said that the greatest act of religious devotion was that we "love the Lord our God with all our heart and with all our soul and with all our mind." (Matthew 22:37) Loving God with our "minds" has to do with thinking clearly about the things of faith and the framework of grace outlined by biblical doctrine. Loving God with our "heart" involves our emotions, and the passions of our lives—allowing them to be reshaped by the glory of the Kingdom.

Loving God with our "soul" is another matter still. It has to do with our wills. Somehow, according to Jesus, whatever it is that drives us onward has to be yoked next to Jesus and become intertwined with his great devotion to the Father.

In the reality of life under the powers that play for our souls that kind of love often means trying to buck the trend and get down the "up" escalator that wants to carry us to a different "Departure" gate. Bill Hybels called it *Descending into Greatness* (Zondervan, 1993), and in his book told stories of those who had found the courage of spirit and the strength of religious will to challenge the patterns of life that had carried them along to places that seemed elevated but lacked eternal substance.

Similarly, when James says to me, "Wayne, humble yourself before the Lord, and he will lift you up," I try to look around me and see which escalator of self-importance I'm riding. Getting down takes a sanctified will.

202

65

Slander Salamander

"Brothers, do not slander one another." (James 4:11)

Robert Fulghum tells of a unique logging practice found among some villagers in the Solomon Islands. If they find a tree that is too big to be felled by their axes they call in a woodsman with special powers. Each morning at dawn he scales that particular tree and, once at the top, screams out a tirade of nasty things against the spirit of the tree. Within a month the tree dies and falls over.

Those villagers are insightful. They know that harsh words can kill the spirit of a living organism. Morris Mandel put it like this: "Gossip is the most deadly microbe. It has neither legs nor wings. It is composed entirely of tales, and most of them have stings."

Moving the Dirt

Gossip is as natural to us as story telling. Gordon Loos remembers his great-uncle George as an incurable gossip, wandering throughout the neighborhood with rumors and whispers. He returned home late for supper once again, in his late 80's, and explained, "I got to talkin' with Mr. Sherwood, an' he jus' couldn't seem to stop listenin'."

That's how we get caught in slander's web. Some years ago the order of service for the Congregational Christian Church in Red Cloud, Nebraska, identified the sermon topic as "**Gossip**," and then declared the next hymn to be "I Love to Tell the Story!" Even "pious" story telling can harm. One wit has quipped that Christians don't gossip; they just share prayer requests!

R. G. LeTourneau, owner of the large earth-moving equipment company reported that one of his salesmen was asked what the "G" on their Model G earthmover stood for. "He was pretty quick on the trigger," said LeTourneau. Without a hesitation he shot back, "Well, I guess the 'G' stands for gossip, because like gossip, this machine moves a lot of dirt and moves it fast!"

Evil Things That Grow

In my younger years we did "scientific" experiments on salamanders. If we cut off a piece of tail, the salamander would grow a new one. If we cut off a leg, the salamander would regenerate itself. No matter how we pared away at our salamanders, they continued to live and crawl on, dropping a piece of dead flesh here and there as they went.

I get that image in my mind every time I think of slander. It looks like a slimy salamander, slithering in the corners, dropping bits of rotting tissue, and growing new "tales" to carry on.

What is the antidote to the virus of slander? I found the research of an Indiana University sociologist very helpful. After three years of investigation Dr. Eder said that a negative word spoken against another human being is not usually itself the starting point of gossip. Many negative judgments we make against other people are true: a man may indeed be "a slob;" a girl may certainly show signs of "conceit;" a driver may well make a "stupid" lane change. Our harsh reaction to these people is not, in and of itself, wrong. Nor does it constitute gossip.

After all, said Dr. Eder, the ability to be moral beings is what defines the soul of humanity over against the animal kingdom. If we are to understand the morality of our own lives we must also be able to evaluate the ethical behavior of others.

Take Your Pick

In fact, according to Dr. Eder, there are always at least three ways in which we can respond to someone's negative judgment about another person, and only one will result in gossip. If we choose not to respond to the initial harsh evaluation, the matter seems most often to die.

Secondly, if we counter the negative judgment with comment that it is probably not correct, the matter usually becomes an argument testing which of us has a more correct view of life. If, however, we affirm the negative judgment and then go on to add another example of our own that seems to confirm it, invariably a loop of gossip began.

Dr. Eder said that the point at which evaluation becomes gossip is only when a second person picks up the negative baton and starts running with it. I find that a helpful analysis. Gossip begins when I take someone else's story and add weight to it. Gossip stops when I carry it no further.

I have a choice in the matter, as James says.

66

A Culture of Litigation

"Anyone who speaks against his brother or judges him speaks against the law and judges it. When you judge the law, you are not keeping it, but sitting in judgment on it. There is only one Lawgiver and Judge, the one who is able to save and destroy. But you—who are you to judge your neighbor?" (James 4:11-12)

One mother tells of a difficult time she was having with her young daughter. They seemed to be going through a testing period, and the girl was doing something wrong nearly every day. The mother would scold and punish, usually with little result. Some days were better than others, but it was a tough time for both of them.

There came a day, however, when things went pretty well. The little girl tried especially hard to be good and to please her mother. That night, after she tucked her daughter in bed, the mother says that she was heading down the stairs when she heard her daughter sobbing into her pillow. Alarmed, the mother went back to the bedroom and asked her daughter what was wrong. Her daughter burst into tears and cried out to her mother, "Haven't I been a little bit good today?"

The mother says, "That question went through me like a knife. I was so quick to correct her when she did wrong, but when she was good I didn't even notice!"

Self-fulfilling Prophecies

James indicates that many of us live like that. We so often see only what we want to see, and what we want to see is the worst in other people.

Some years ago a psychologist named Aldrich published a fascinating article. He had worked in social services, spending most of his time with teenagers who had been arrested for shoplifting or other theft. Aldrich interviewed them to find out how they had come to this. He also talked with the parents, attempting to discover how they had handled the problem from the first time they knew about it.

Over the years he kept records of his interviews, noting that they seemed to separate into two types. One group of teens became repeat offenders and showed up in the criminal justice system again and again. The other was a collection of those who were with him one time and then stayed straight.

He came to the conclusion that there were basically two different ways that parents responded to the initial shoplifting incident. Some parents confronted their children with words like this: "Now we know what you're like! You're a thief! We're going to be watching you now, buddy! Don't think you can get away with this again!"

The other group of parents usually said something like this: "Tom, that wasn't like you at all! We'll have to go back to the store and clear this thing up, but then it's done with, okay? What you did was wrong. You know that it was wrong. But we're sure you won't do it again."

Aldrich said that the parents who assumed the worst usually got the worst, and the parents who assumed the best most often got the best.

Eyes of Love

Much that pretends to be Christian religion seems to have a rather negative view of the human spirit. Although the Bible speaks prophetically in judgment against blatant sinfulness, there are also many passages in scripture that tell of God's delight in his children. More than that, the Fruit of the Spirit, which the apostle Paul says becomes the way of life for someone who is loved by God, is itself "love, joy, peace, patience, kindness, goodness, faithfulness, gentleness and self-control" (Galatians 5:22-23). As

207

God looks with tender eyes at us, so we are encouraged to view others with grace.

That can be a powerful influence in a person's life. One writer tells of attending a business conference where awards were being given for outstanding achievements during the past fiscal year. A woman was called to the podium to receive the company's top honor. Clutching her trophy, she beamed out at the crowd of over 3000 people. Yet in that moment of triumph, she had eyes for only one person. She looked directly at her supervisor, a woman named Joan.

The award-winner told of the difficult times that she had gone through only a few years earlier. She had experienced personal problems, and, for a time her work had suffered. Some people turned away from her, counting it a liability to be seen with her. Others wrote her off as a loser in the company.

The worst part was that she felt they were right. She had stopped at Joan's desk several times with a letter of resignation in her hand. She knew she was a failure.

But Joan said, "Let's just wait a little bit longer." And Joan said, "Give it one more try." And Joan said, "I never would have hired you if I didn't think you could handle it!"

The woman's voice broke. Tears streamed down her cheeks as she softly said, "Joan believed in me more than I believed in myself!"

From Prosecutor to Prism

Isn't that the message of the Gospel? Isn't that the story of the Bible? That God believed in us while we were still sinners, while we were still failures, while we were at the point in our lives that we couldn't seem to make it on our own?

Sometimes we need the straightedge of God's law in order to see how bent we are. But sometimes, when the law is a mirror of our great God, it helps us learn to smile at others like he has at us.

67

Busy People

"Now listen, you who say, 'Today or tomorrow we will go to this or that city, spend a year there, carry on business and make money.'" (James 4:13)

There are times when I feel as if Robert Louis Stevenson was talking about me when he wrote, "He sows hurry and reaps indigestion." I don't think I'm alone in that.

I remember the story of a man in New York City who kept a very regular schedule. He lived in an apartment and worked his day to the clock. At 6:13 every morning the alarm went off. By 6:27 he had showered and shaved. Breakfast was finished precisely at 6:42. He stepped out of his apartment at 6:46, caught the elevator down at 6:47, and headed out the building for the ferry at 6:50. The ferry left at 7:10, and the man usually had a minute and a half to get himself a newspaper and a cup of coffee as he walked on. The rest of his day ticked off in routine.

But a power outage one night stalled his wake-up alarm. When his internal clock finally shook him to his senses, his wristwatch glared 6:32. He was late! With a flurry of fuss he scrambled to make it to the ferry. Exerting superhuman effort he managed to run down to the dock just as the ferry was about 6 feet out in the water. Never stopping to think, he raced to the edge and took a flying leap onto the ferry deck. He made it!

A deck hand came over to congratulate him on the fine jump. Then the boatman added, "I'm not sure why you wanted to do that, sir. You could have waited until we pulled in at the dock. It's a lot safer."

In his rush, the man had gotten ahead of himself and beat the ferry in!

Steady Now!

Life is a rush for many of us, even though time itself is a fixed commodity we all share equally. For the most part we pass through time at the same rate as Napoleon did, and Caesar Augustus, and David and Abraham. Yes, the earth is slowing in its rotation all the time, say the scientists, but it happens at such an incredibly insignificant rate that no one could tell when the atmosphere has caused enough friction to add even a micro-second to our calendars.

Still, our awareness of time changes as we grow older. If a four-year-old has to wait a year before starting kindergarten, that amounts to a quarter of her life. In fact, it is probably about as long as her whole memory.

The last term of elementary school seems to pass much more quickly since, at that point in a child's life, a year is about 1/10 of a lifetime. Take that same year to college or university, and a student realizes that an academic year is only 1/20 of her conscious memory. When middle age sets in, the passing of four seasons becomes a very limited segment of our total life spans.

Every successive year is a smaller portion for us over against its predecessors, simply because we have gone through more hours and days and years and ages by the time we arrived at this point in time. That is true at 5 and it is true at 55. For that reason, according to researchers, time seems constantly to keep speeding up for all of us.

Killing Time

But that is only half of the story. Sometimes, in spite of the fact that time is speeding up for us, it seems to drag and lag and stagnate as well. Our lives can be like the motto of World War II soldiers:

"Hurry up and wait!" Time passes, but waiting kills it: waiting out retirement; waiting for family to come and visit; waiting to hear the verdict of the medical examination; waiting for the crisis in our marriage to find some resolution. Those are the hard moments and days when we are just "killing time." Unfortunately, time never dies.

Time matters in the church. The clock of eternity keeps ticking, and this year will bring us one portion closer to the time when time will abruptly be swallowed up by eternity as Jesus returns. That is why we count years with the letters A.D., short for the Latin term *anno domine*, which means "the year of our Lord."

The Shortest Way Through Time

Whether we are homebodies or global frequent-flier miles collectors we all must travel through time. Some years ago a small town newspaper in England ran a contest seeking the best answer to the question, "What is the shortest way to London?" Hundreds of entries poured in, most with maps or drawings of short cuts along the highway systems of that region. Some wrote of the time it took them to travel each route, explaining that certain routes were faster even if they measured slightly longer in distance.

Although most people were surprised at the winning entry selected by the judges, all agreed that it was, indeed, the best answer to the question, "What is the shortest way to London?" The prize went to the woman who wrote: "The shortest way to London is in good company."

She was right. The shortest way to get from here to there is always in the company of those who care about me, and who share a warmth of good camaraderie.

That is really what the church is all about. Whatever else we are doing with our time as we travel from birth to eternity, we need to do it in good company. We are in the business of building relationships, building community, building a network of care and compassion, of laughter and love, of hands that hold and arms that embrace.

Recently a couple told me with delight about the way they had found community at their church. Another young man told me of his great appreciation for his friend who first helped him find his way in a dark time, and then who brought him to worship services to enjoy the company of others seeking grace. A woman said that she had stopped participating in anything social, but the people and the ministries of a neighboring congregation kept drawing her back.

The shortest way to travel through time, whether we are busy or bored, is in good company. Almost always after we have enjoyed an evening of friendship we say, "My, how time flies!"

68

Finishing Our Education

"Why, you do not even know what will happen tomorrow. What is your life? You are a mist that appears for a little while and then vanishes. Instead, you ought to say, 'If it is the Lord's will, we will live and do this or that.'" (James 4:14-15)

Charles Eliot was president of Harvard University for 40 years at the turn of the 20th century. One evening colleagues at the school were honoring him with a dinner, and toasting his accomplishments. One fellow raised his glass and said, "Since you became president, Harvard has become a storehouse of knowledge!"

Eliot modestly replied, "What you say is true, but I can claim little credit for it. It is simply that the first year students bring so much, and the graduates take so little away!"

In a similar way early Amherst College president George Harris lamented, in his opening speech of the school year, "Ah, I intended to give you some advice, but now I remember how much is left over from last year unused!"

Precious Commodity

Education is a precious thing. We have long valued good schools and continuing skills development on the job. And, like Eliot and Harris, we tend to pity those who have opportunities to grow and learn but fail to take advantage.

Watching an infant mature through the stages of life is an awesome thing. The size of the body changes, although the torso and limbs grow much more rapidly than the head. That doesn't mean, however, that little is happening in the slow-growing skull. The opposite is, in fact, the case. Our brains are almost like sponges, taking in information as fast as our senses can process it.

What is most striking about the way that we mature, however, is its global integration. Muscles tone, coordination develops, the will becomes stronger, facts are memorized and analogies unfold that make it possible for us to apply old learning to new situations. Growth is a never-ending process of insight deepened through experience and applied to expression. It is difficult to track the process of maturation, but easy to tell when it is missing. No one complains about children being childlike, but the childishness of adults is nearly always panned.

Practices of Faith

So too in the Christian life, according to James. There is a child-like exuberance that energizes every room where a new child of God enters. We delight in the amazing grace of the faith-birthing process, and are thrilled with the stories of change and transformation that happen when God comes home to live in a life of one of his children.

But the stories of conversion are not enough to sustain faith or to explore the wonder of life in the Promised Land. Faith needs to grow. Horizons need to expand. Insights need to connect and skills of service need to be put to use. Most of all, dependence on God needs to multiply.

Growth in the Christian faith happens in several directions at once. As we move on from our first profession of faith we all need to increase our knowledge of the teachings of the Bible and the insights of the church's theology. Second, we need to develop our ability to understand our spiritual gifts and passions in order to take our place in the Christ-service of his Body, the Church. Third, we need to learn the vocabulary of faith so that we can communicate intelligently to others of the things God is doing inside of us and the vision he has for the world and eternity. Fourth, we need constantly to groom our understanding of the meaning and character of relationships so that we can live as supportive social beings. Fifth, we need to foster the intuitive dimension of our personalities in order to catch the wind of the Spirit and sail the seas of grace. Sixth, we need to strengthen our wills to be able to keep us compassionately strong through times of great stress and upheaval. Seventh, we need to deepen love as we practice care, living as God's signs of new life.

The old hymn says, "Change and decay in all around I see." As James notes, the changing face of life creates a kind of mist in which we can wander aimlessly, or become silly in our self-importance. Yet there is also a lot of health in the changes that take place among people who are always growing. The only time we truly stop changing is when we die. More than that, the only time we truly grow well is when we grow in trust.

69

Service with More than a Smile

"As it is, you boast and brag. All such boasting is evil. Anyone, then, who knows the good he ought to do and doesn't do it, sins." (James 4:16-17)

A friend of mine stopped at a small diner one evening wanting a quick cup of coffee as he took a break between pastoral visits. There were only two others at tables around the room, yet the waitress was anything but prompt in getting to him. In fact, for almost ten minutes as my friend sat there, an angry male voice was pounding away in the kitchen, verbally beating away on the young waitress.

Finally appearing, she was visibly shaking, her eyes tearing and face puffy with pain. My friend ordered a 50-cent cup of coffee (this was quite a few years ago!) and she brought it without ever meeting his eyes or uttering a word. He wanted cream with his coffee, but startled by all of the earlier commotion he had forgotten to ask the waitress to bring him some. Now he didn't have the heart to trouble her further, so he gulped the black java, paid for the coffee at the register, and exited to his next appointment.

And he left a $10 tip.

He told me the story as we were comparing horror stories of bad restaurant service one day. He didn't wait around to see how the waitress would react, he said, because he gave the $10 out of compassion and empathy, and not from a desire to be thanks for his generosity. He just felt so bad about the way the young woman had been orally whipped by her boss that he needed to do something to help balance the books of justice and mercy in the universe.

Service with an Open Palm?

There are all sorts of reasons we may be extra nice to people: altruism, guilt, camaraderie, love, or even the need to be recognized for our great spirits. And in our world "service" has become a selling point. **ServiceMaster** Corporation has grown astronomically by offering to clean those places we don't want to clean ourselves. Shopkeepers put staff members through Dale Carnegie courses in order to get them to earn business with politeness and smiles. Sloganeers publish these "rule cards" for companies:

Rules for Business
1. The Customer is always right!
2. See Rule #1.

While all of this may be nice, creating something of the "kinder, gentler society" that former president George Bush longed for, and even though it support some of the teachings of the church (expressing the "Fruit of the Spirit," for instance—love, joy, peace, patience, kindness, goodness, faithfulness, gentleness, self-control), the selling of service can actually detract from the central message of the gospel. Jesus came, he told his disciples, not to be served but to serve others. Paul encourages us to gain the "mind of Christ," which he says has to do with initiating care for others. James earlier writes that religion itself is about looking after the needs of widow and the orphan. In other words, the church ought to be a place of service not because it "sells" in our society but because service is essential to the very character of God's people.

One of the questions we would ask one another in my accountability group was this: "What service have you done for someone during the past month?" Often we found ourselves consuming our time with job demands and family activities. We could go a month or longer without ever taking time to simply be Jesus for others around us.

Give What You Need

James' words remind us that our goal in life should be to "do good." It is clear that he means we should learn to serve others. True service in the Kingdom of God is far more than working for tips. It is a way of making the heart of Jesus real to others.

A speaker was once accosted at a public forum by a divorced woman who told of the raw deal she had gotten in life—left by her husband, untrained for high-paying jobs, smoking heavily to calm her nerves, burdened by sole care of young children. "Who's going to help me?" she demanded. "I'm overweight and washed up! Nobody wants to be around me anymore! Even my 'friends' find convenient reasons to avoid me!"

"What do you need most?" asked the speaker. She responded with a list of wants—someone to sit with the children so she could get out again and feel like an adult; someone to cook a meal for her now and again; someone to listen to her when she needed to vent. Every need was obvious.

"Now," said the speaker, "give what you need!"

"What?" she demanded.

"Give what you need," he said again. "Yes, it is wrong what your former husband did to you, and yes, your situation is tough. But the most important need you have is to be an adult human being and the most effective way of finding that in yourself is to give to others what you know you need yourself."

It was a watershed moment, and silence filled the auditorium. Then life buzzed on.

Make Me a Blessing

Six months later that speaker was stopped by a woman who reminded him of the incident. "You were right," she said. "I started looking at people and seeing their needs as well as mine, and somehow I found that we needed each other. You wouldn't believe all the friends I have today!"

You and I can't love the whole human race—our spirits would fade in sheer exhaustion. But we can nurture community in small ways among those near us. And we can give to several other people the little things of life that we know we need ourselves.

Every time we gather for worship in our church we close the celebration with a pronouncement of God's blessing:

> **The Lord bless you and keep you!**
>
> **The Lord make his face shine upon you and be gracious to you!**
>
> **The Lord turn his face toward you and give you peace!** (Numbers 6:24-26)

In truth, God's blessing for the person standing near you may well be you. So when God blesses that other person next Sunday, stretch your hands and heart of care to her to make it possible for God's blessing to reach her.

70

Death by Dissociation

"Now listen, you rich people, weep and wail because of the misery that is coming upon you. Your wealth has rotted, and moths have eaten your clothes. Your gold and silver are corroded. Their corrosion will testify against you and eat your flesh like fire. You have hoarded wealth in the last days. Look! The wages you failed to pay the workmen who mowed your fields are crying out against you. The cries of the harvesters have reached the ears of the Lord Almighty. You have lived on earth in luxury and self-indulgence. You have fattened yourselves in the day of slaughter. You have condemned and murdered innocent men, who where not opposing you." (James 5:1-6)

One of the most widely viewed television programs of all time was the Fox-TV special "Who Wants to Marry a Millionaire?" Fifty women from around North America were brought together for two-hours of interviews and beauty-pageant parading while a mysterious multi-millionaire sat cloistered in a booth observing by way of monitors. Friends and family of the tycoon assisted him in rating the ten semi-finalists and five finalists until the big moment arrived. With five women now clad in designer wedding dresses standing at attention before thousands in the auditorium and 23 million network viewers the man who controlled all the shots stepped forward to grab one woman and wed her immediately before an authorized judge. The newly married pair danced their wedding tryst on a stage surrounded by 49 losers while credits rolled, signaling the end of the program.

Name That Game

There was a great deal of controversy in the days that followed. The woman quit her nursing job and disappeared from her family and friends. Investigators dredged up a woman-beating indictment issued years earlier against the millionaire. Moralists wrote columns about the scandal of television rating games, denouncing Fox for pulling off something the other networks wished they would have thought of first.

There was little said, however, about the strangeness of money itself that made this weird situation possible in the first place. An end-run was done around every element of courtship simply because one person had the financial resources to say so. While the marriage was arranged as completely as that of Isaac and Rebekkah, there was no wise parent or trusted friend who spent considerable time appraising the unknown person until a reasonable match could be made based on personality and values. Furthermore, the "winner" was truly a financial winner, with a great deal of wealth tagged to her new wedding ring. At the same time, the multi-millionaire was protected from financial ruin by prenuptuals that guaranteed no sharing of resources.

In other words, the woman was bought like a prostitute for a one-night stand and no relationship was secured by it. The only person capable of pulling off something like this was a wealthy man. A poor man would have had actually to court a woman in order to move toward marriage. Wealth insulated the multi-millionaire from the messy stuff of making a relationship work. One day he bought a mansion. Another day he bought a yacht. That day he bought a wife.

Insulated by Wealth

Some time ago June Fletcher wrote a perceptive article in the *Wall Street Journal*. "Behind walls, millions seek havens," she said (February 2, 1996, p. B8). There is a mushrooming demand for "gated communities" in the United States, according to Fletcher. People put fences around their communities and push away those not like them. One of the main reasons, according to Fletcher, was outlined in a massive study done by Philip Langdon. He said, "Although people are motivated by concerns about crime and intrusion, there's also prestige in walling yourself off from others. It says that you've risen in the pecking order."

The insulation of wealth invades churches as well as neighborhoods. A friend of mine was director of a Christian social agency some years ago. He said that the goal of his organization was to connect those in need with congregations where the needs could be met. People were referred to Christians who had the resources to meet one or two small needs. Too often, however, said my friend, the deacons of those congregations would call him asking that no more referrals be made. They would like to take up an offering, or perhaps do a food drive for a few weeks. But they did not want to have to deal with people in need directly. One pastor told my friend that his congregation was not into helping people directly. "Why don't you tell us how much you need to operate next month," said the pastor, "and we'll cut you a check. We've got a lot of money in our Benevolence account."

James seems incredibly hard-nosed about the nastiness of wealthy people. Some want to explain away his views by blaming it on some unusual dynamics of James' home town or a bad experience of his childhood. Yet it is impossible to ignore the reality that wealth isolates some people from others, and insulates some hearts from true compassion. As the wealth of a congregation increases it tends to want to play the "Who Wants to Marry a Millionaire?" game rather than invest time and effort in the courtship process of walking with those in need.

More than Money

When Clarence Jordan, the author of the *Cottonpatch Bible*, started a Christian community on a farm in the south, many who admired his spiritual wisdom came to apply. A very wealthy woman approached him one day, begging a place among the group. Jordan agreed to receive her on one condition. "First sell everything you have and give it away," he told her.

She was willing to sell everything, she said, and then to give the money to Jordan's Christian community. He refused. "Don't you need money to run this place?" she asked.

"We certainly do," he replied. "We would love to have your money. But if you gave us your money and you became a member of our community, your money would keep you apart from everyone else. We would all know that we owed you a lot, and we would never see you as one of us."

He was right. James is not begging for rich people to make a donation to the church. He is pointing out the same thing Jesus did in the Sermon on the Mount—money is a god and until we deal with its power we cannot find our place in the Kingdom of God.

Money doesn't heal. Money doesn't cure. Wealth can't protect or assist. Only people can help people. Only God and make life work. And he will never appear on a television show called, "Who Wants to Marry God Today?" He values us far too much to ever do a silly thing like that.

71

Waiting or Wilting?

"Be patient, then, brothers, until the Lord's coming." (James 5:7)

A friend of mine was awakened suddenly on a Saturday morning by a telephone call across three time zones. His brother had been injured and was hospitalized in the critical care unit with a cracked skull and a swelling brain. My friend langored in helplessness. No airplane could get him to his brother's side before either the injury might prove fatal or the swelling would subside and the emergency pass. Enforced patience drummed him with nervous fret, a burden he did not want to bear.

A Lesson We Don't Want to Learn

Patience is a tough virtue, slipping from our grasp in the moment of demand. It always races with Road Runner while we are stymied in the dust with Wile E. Coyote, never catching up no matter what Acme technology we employ. Stephen Winward says that at his mother's knee he learned a poem that has proved perennially true:

Patience is a virtue: possess it if you can!

Seldom in a woman, and never in a man.

My own parents used to tell us, "All good things come to those who wait." While that may have been true in the past it hardly seems to apply any more. We seem systematically to have beaten the need for waiting. We buy instant foods, and "nuke" them to serving temperature in microwave ovens. Our satellite dishes and Internet search engines bring immediate access to news and information from around the world. We pop pain killers to evaporate our aches, so we don't even have to deal with the whys of our hurts. If we see something we like, instant credit grants us immediate possession.

Frustration Station

Still, there are things that we can't control, and these keep the fires of desire burning the paper house of patience in our souls. Dianna Ross and the Supremes sang about it in their Motown testimony:

> **I need love, love, to ease my mind.**
>
> **I need to find, find someone to call mine.**
>
> **But momma said, "You can't hurry love,**
>
> **No, you'll just have to wait."**
>
> **She said, "Love don't come easy, it's a game of give and take.**
>
> **You can't hurry love—no, you'll just have to wait.**
>
> **You gotta just give it time, no matter how long it takes."**
>
> **But how many heartaches must I stand**
>
> **Before I find a love to let me live again?**
>
> **How long must I wait, how much more can I take,**
>
> **Before loneliness will cause my heart to break?**
>
> **Now I can't bear to live my life alone.**
>
> **I grow impatient for a love to call my own.**

It is the ache of loneliness and the pain of frustration that too often hold us aloof from patience. Today, again, I received a letter from a wife who's life has been turned up-side down by a marriage gone sour and the complicated pains it causes each day. "I'm so lonely," she shouts in print, punctuating her cry with exclamation points. I've spent time in her impatient circle. You have too.

James indicates that patience is a religious matter, and ties it to our understanding of time and eternity. "Be patient," he says, "until the Lord's coming." That is a tall order. The church in first century Thessalonica was trying to be "patient until the Lord's coming," and Paul had to tell the people to get back to work (2 Thessalonians 2-3) rather than constantly scanning the horizon. Others in the early church fully expected Jesus to return before the elderly apostle John died. After all, Jesus had hinted at that possibility in his final seaside morning picnic with his disciples (John 21).

Eschatological Expectation

Throughout history people have tried to run ahead of patience by pretending it wasn't needed, that the world would end before they did. The Millerites and the Seventh Day Adventists announced Judgment Day watches several times over. People climbed trees and sat on rooftops in all-night vigils. But starry skies never split with angelic celebration and the dreams died with graying dawn. So too did the patience.

A neighboring farmer in my boyhood community was captured by one of these millennial preachers. He sold his farm, bought a motor home, and traveled with his family in caravan with a dozen others chasing the preacher on a whirlwind tour of North America, spreading the news of Kingdom come. Six months later they circled the motor homes in Texas and waited. And waited. And waited.

When Jesus refused to do a command curtain call on their schedule, the motor homes began to drift away. The prophetic band broke up, disillusioned with a near-sighted preacher, and our neighbor sneaked back to Minnesota in shame. He died a short while later, tired of patience that gave out before promise.

This is the religious dimension of patience that James urges and we find hard to manage. Our world is imperfect, with corners that bump knees and scorpions that poison hands. We get lonely, we get pained; we struggle to survive and are old in body before our youthful ideals get a chance to catch up. We try to find a little comfort and come away addicted to work or booze or drugs or sex always far short of heaven.

The patience of waiting is tied to our understanding of how time will get resolved into eternity. If there is no God outside the system, we are stuck with cycles of repetition, crushed beneath recurring tasks and tedium that never ends. But if there is a God who has promised to interrupt history with healing and hope and harmony, we wait with expectation.

My friend's brother died from his head injuries. Now my friend waits with the patience of James for the coming of Jesus. He is confident that then he will see his brother again, according to the promise of scripture. Without that promise he could not be patient. In an impatient world his is a remarkable hope. A religious hope. A patient hope.

72

Pastoral Perspective

"See how the farmer waits for the land to yield its valuable crop and how paitent he is for the autumn and spring rains. You too, be patient and stand firm, because the Lord's coming is near." (James 5:7-8)

Are farmers more patient than the rest of us?

I grew up on a farm and can't say that rural folks have a corner on the patience market. They seemed pretty ordinary, and just as likely to grow frustrated as others. In fact, during my boyhood many farmers joined a fledgeling association called the National Farmers Organization (NFO). The NFO grew rapidly and became incredibly violent, capturing media and government attention with roadblocks, illegal port embargoes, and even rifle shootings, in an attempt to lower farm taxes and raise grain subsidies. Farmers in those days bristled with impatience.

Field of Dreams

There are, of course, always the quiet ones in every group. A farmer in our area won a million dollar lottery. At that time a million dollars was an incredible amount of money. News reporters flocked to his yard to capitalize on this great human interest story. "What are you going to do with all your money?" they asked.

"Oh, I don't know," shrugged the man, caught off guard by the public's attention. "I reckon I'll just keep farming till it's gone."

He probably did!

Farmers are not more patient than others. Yet in one way they are forced into a waiting role that others may not experience. Once the seed is in the ground they have no way to make it grow faster. They cannot speed up the natural processes of production.

I remember the first time that our family planted a little vegetable garden behind our house. We had a few green plastic flower pots in the garage, so each of our girls got to plant her own seed, either a bean or a pea. That was fun, but then came the tedium of waiting. How can you be sure that the seed is growing when you can't see it? Every day our youngest daughter wanted to dig it up and check it out.

A farmer knows you can't do that. If you dig up the seeds they will never grow. If you pull out the young plants, they will die. In order to get the produce from the field you have to wait for the seasons to run their course.

This is the patience that James urges in our lives. We will never be able to control everything around us. We will never have the ability to force it all into our time schedules. There will always be things that deny us that right.

Hardscrabble Farm

How do you cope, for instance, when you've built up your business but the economy takes a nose dive and you're wiped out? It wasn't your fault. It wasn't your neighbor's fault. It just happened.

What do you do when cancer invades your body and all your planning and hoping and dreaming has to press itself into ten months? How do you deal with it?

How can you carry on when a little incident in the Middle East sends the whole world to war? Soldiers die, governments crumble, and the clouds of doom hang everywhere. What's left in life?

There are things beyond our control, and they can prove quite frustrating. A little girl went fishing with her dad one day. Even though she didn't like worms the morning was wonderful because her dad fixed them on her hook. There they sat... Half-an-hour, no bites. An hour, no bites. After an hour-and-a-half she threw down her pole and cried, "I quit!"

"Why? What's the matter?" asked her dad.

"Oh, nuthin'" she said, "except that I can't get waited on!"

What do you do when you can't get waited on? In 1938 Adolph Hitler said, "My patience is now at an end," and he pushed the world to war. And sometimes that's the way we cope with things in life we can't handle. We fight or we quit. We lash out and hurt someone else, or we drop out and commit suicide.

The Patience of Perspective

That is where the lesson of the farmer becomes so important. When the crops are growing things are beyond your control. That doesn't mean you sit around doing nothing. Patience is not a cop-out or a drop-out. The farmer is still busy weeding the rows and preparing the machinery for harvest. He knows what he can't do and also what he can. And he has learned to be content with that.

In essence, the farmer has learned perspective. He has learned to stand outside the system long enough to understand the processes at work in the system. And, he has learned that even if he cannot control the system, God can. God will bring the rains. God will keep the temperature on planet earth within the range necessary for human and plant life to survive. God will balance the droughts and floods so that there will be fruitful as well as lean years.

No one is born a farmer. It takes years to gain the sensitivities necessary to read the ways of nature with plants and animals.

So too with faith. Patience grows in those who have taken the time to watch the Master Farmer at work with his world. They know that every season brings its stresses and sorrows. But they also know that those who wait with hope will not be disappointed in the harvest yield.

73

Fostering Forebearance

"Don't grumble against each other, brothers, or you will be judged. The Judge is at the door! Brothers,

as an example of patience in the face of suffering, take the prophets who spoke in the name of the Lord."

(James 5:9-10)

One medical study seems to indicate that chronic complainers tend to live longer than people who have a mild and pleasant disposition. In other words, if you are irritable and cranky you have a better chance of living to be a hundred.

But one person, at least, has questioned those findings. He says complainers do not necessarily live longer; it just *seems* like it to those around them! One woman who prayed for patience found her world suddenly inundated with clumsy and trying people. Patience is not something one can order up on demand, but a choice that grows out of difficult relationships.

Cruel People

That is probably why James points to the prophets of the Old Testament as an example of the practice of patience. Think of Jeremiah who argued with God about not wanting to be a prophet. He just wanted to live with his family and friends. Yet the urgency of love for God and his community demanded that he speak the truth. For his efforts he was dumped into a slimy pit and barely kept alive on moldy bread. Isaiah, who felt the passion of care, speaking of "comfort" (Isaiah 40:1), was eventually hacked to death with a sword. Amos found his name on the king's "most wanted" posters. Ahab and Jezebel were forever making the lives of Elijah and Elisha miserable.

People can be cruel to people. Brothers get in a tiff about family money and don't speak to each other for years. Sisters-in-law become spiteful and mean. Business associates use gossip to destroy each other while competing for honors at the office. Husbands abuse their wives and children push the sarcasm buttons that dig at their parents.

In the sixteenth century Dr. Thomas Cooper edited a major new dictionary of the English language. For eight years he worked on it, collecting notes, writing definitions, and researching sources. Then one day, while he was out of the house, his wife decided to finish a fight they had been having by buring every paper in his study. People can be cruel to each other.

Chosing Patience

How do we deal with cruel people? How do we cope with those who do us wrong? Our human nature says "Strike back in kind! Live by the motto: Do unto others before they have a chance to do it to you!" In politics, in the church, in our homes it is all the same thing—name calling, mud slinging, bitterness and sarcasm. Others did it to us, and we'll do it back.

But James tells of another way. The word translated as "patience" in verse 10 really means "long-suffering." It means taking a long time to get angry. It means not paying back in kind when someone has been cruel to me. It means refusing to let the other person determine how I am going to react.

When baseball player Jackie Robinson was signed on by the Brooklyn Dodgers in 1947 he was the first African-American on a major league team. People were cruel to him, spitting racial jokes and smearing him with sick humor. Even some of his own team mates tortured him from day to day.

Manager Branch Rickey knew it would be tough for Robinson, but he also knew that Robinson was a Christian. He said he wanted a player with guts enough *not* to fight back. That is what Robinson did. He was "long suffering." He had patience enough not to pay back in kind. He lived what James talks about here.

Caring Perseverance

Sometimes people mistake patience in others as a sign of weakness. Ambrose Bierce, in his famous *Devil's Dictionary*, defined patience as "a minor form of despair disguised as a virtue." In other words, patience is for wimps, for the helpless and the hopeless, for those who have no backbone. They pretend to be patient, but really they are just too weak to fight back.

Biblical patience, however, isn't weakness. It is, rather, a kind of strength that chooses the weapons of combat, determining to fight cruelty with love and mean-spiritedness with compassion. The prophets were no wimps. Hosea *chose* to love a woman who was unfaithful to him, echoing God's passion for his wayward people. Jeremiah *chose* to stay with the poor people of Jerusalem even though they ridiculed him, simply because he cared so much about them. "Look at the prophets," says James.

I know a couple whose only son was killed by a drunk driver who was driving without a license and had no insurance. Friends and lawyers urged them to sue the man and his wealthy parents for all they were worth. The courts would gladly judge this travesty in their favor.

"No," they replied. "We refuse to live that way." Instead, with patient love, they slowly built a relationship with the young wastrel. Eventually they take him from prison into their home, and allow him to become another son to them in place of the one who was lost to them under this man's car.

Is patience weak? Certainly not in these quiet folk. They have proved it to be stronger than revenge. Patience is not putting up with something because we have no way out; rather it is choosing to stick with people and continuing to love them even when we could become angry or mean or hurtful, even when we could just turn our back and walk away.

Somehow that sounds a lot like God!

74

The Patience of Job

"As you know, we consider blessed those who have persevered. You have heard of Job's perseverance and have seen what the Lord finally brought about. The Lord is full of compassion and mercy." (James 5:11)

Do you remember the story of Job? He was one of the wealthiest men in the ancient world, with houses and servants and treasures. He had more of everything than any person could covet.

Job was also a devout man, careful to renew his relationship with God each day. It seems, in fact, that God was rather proud of Job. When Satan came calling one time God bragged to him about Job. "Have you seen my servant Job?" he asked. "Now *there* is a man whose heart you will never own!"

Wagering

Satan wasn't so sure. He has cracked a lot of tough nuts in his time, and he too on Job as a special challenge. "Sure, Job loves you," Satan said to God. "But that's because you've bought his soul. You give him everything he wants. Why shouldn't he serve you? Even *I* would do that!"

That's when the wagering began, according to the Old Testament book. God gives Satan permission to take everything away from Job, stipulating only that Satan cannot harm Job's own body.

So Job loses everything—his children, his flocks, his buildings, his servants. He becomes as poor as a church mouse. Yet still Job loves God and serves him openly.

The wagering in heaven heats up, and Satan gets one more shot at Job in Round Two. He may touch Job's body without killing him. Job begins to writhe in pain. And Satan touches Job's mind so that he can no longer clearly hear God's whisper of love. Job is all alone. His wife calls him stupid, his friends call him a liar and a sinner, and the world doesn't even call him anymore. Outside Job's horizons have collapsed. Inside he has become an echo chamber of despair. Where is God?

Wasting

That is the hardest challenge in life, isn't it? I remember sitting with a mother in a hospital corridor, praying for the life of her daughter. The young woman was just beyond her teen years, and only a dozen months into marriage to a wonderful man. When the doctor assisted her delivery of her first child he nicked something with his knife. Now she was turning every shade of yellow and gray, and had been flown half-way across the country to get the best medical attention possible.

The mother was unconsoled. When we prayed she felt no peace, and could not find God. And for three hours we watched her daughter's life slip away.

The mother stopped going to church. The young husband grew angry and didn't know how to care for his baby child. Where was God?

Elie Wiesel endured the horror of the Nazi death camps. He watched women and children herded into gas chambers. He cried with men beaten down by cruel soldiers. He saw a young boy hanging on a gallows. "Where is God?" he cried.

The Armenians are one of earth's oldest civilizations. They turned to Christ in the early history of the Church. Devout people. God-fearing people. Church-going people. Yet other nations have slaughtered them, nearly wiping them off the map. Where is God?

The question of Job is asked in every generation: "Where are you God?" And often, as with Job, the only answer is silence. The promises of Scripture become dead fantasies. The Holy Spirit leaves and the heart grows chilly. The newspapers report events that make no sense. Where is God? Where is God when a child dies? Where is God when a mother is snatched from her family? Where is God when nuclear reactors melt down and airplanes crash and mines collapse? Where is God?

Waiting

And Satan looks down from heaven with glee. He knows that he has Job now. He knows that we will never get out of this one. He knows the cards in his hand are the winning draw. Can faith remain when God is silent? Can trust carry on when there seems to be no one at the other end of the line?

"No!" shouts Satan. But *he* doesn't have the last world.

"Yes!" whispers Job. "Even though I cannot see him, even though I do not understand what is happening, even though every human wisdom tells me God's not there, I *know* that my Redeemer lives, and with these eyes I shall see him!"

That is the deepest level of patience possible. James calls it perseverance. Job loves God not for what he gets out of it, but because it is the only way life itself makes sense. We trust in God not because we always feel the wonder of his presence, but because, even in his absense, there is truly nowhere else to turn.

This is the patience of Job. It is the perseverance at the heart of the Christian faith. It is trust at its most profound level.

No one, of course, can explain it, at least not with words. Those of us who have struggled in that black pit can never really share the experience. We can talk about it later, when God seems closer again. But it is the awful agony of faith when we stand undressed and all alone.

Wisdom

Years ago Dr. Arthur Gossip preached a sermon he called "When Life Tumbles in, What Then?" He brought that message on the first Sunday he returned to the pulpit of his congregation after his beloved wife had suddenly died. This is how he ended the sermon: "Our hearts are very frail, and there are places where the road is very steep and very lonely. ...standing in the roaring Jordan, cold with its dreadful chill and very conscious of its terror, of its rushing, I... call back to you who one day will have your turn to cross it, 'Be of good cheer, my brothers, for I feel the bottom and it is sound.'"

Somehow, by the grace of God, the perseverance of patience carries us through, and we know the end of the matter as did Job. God will never leave us alone forever. He will answer our questions in time. He will resolve the problems of life and give us a future that Satan could never manufacture. "The Lord is full of compassion and mercy," says James. And the patience of faith carries us through, until we know that better than we know ourselves.

75

Words with Power

"Above all, my brothers, do not swear—not by heaven or by earth or by anything else. Let your 'Yes' be yes, and your 'No,' no, or you will be condemned." (James 5:12)

In this age of automated communications I now and again get computer-generated mailings. One that appeared recently made me smile. "Dear Mr. Wayne Bronwer," it began, "you are someone special. You are an individual who thinks for yourself. That's why I've decided, Mr. Bronwer, to make you, and you alone, this very special offer. The enclosed form has your name on it, Mr. Bronwer, yours alone..."

It went on, asking me to sign my name so that I and all who live at my address could benefit from this once-in-a-lifetime offer. Meanwhile, the letter consistently spelled my name wrong.

There was great discontinuity between that attempt to be personal and chummy with me, and at the same time doing business through a very impersonal automated mail service. No matter how often my name was used it was like a slap in the face from someone flashing a fake smile.

ID Tags

Our names are our badges of identity. We want people to treat us with respect, and it begins with the way they use our names. Before World War II there were 14 listing under "Hitler" in the New York city telephone directory. After the war the entire list had disappeared. None of those families wanted any

238

longer to be identified with a name that had become a symbol of international evil.

On the other hand, each year for the last several decades, when the list of most popular names for newborns in North America is published, the first two or three names each for boys and girls have been stage names for popular daytime television dramas. Mothers hope their offspring will look and sound and act like the folks whose lives they peep at for an hour daily.

Names have power. We know that the way we speak names to one another opens a process of power-brokering between us. I can use my wife's name to tell her how much I love her. Or, in another frame of mind, I can speak her name almost like scathing judgment. Parents use power over children for good or ill in the manner they speak names. Co-workers connect or poison relationships with names. In society the names of politicians become banners of goodness or talismans of arrogance and stupidity. One person who has my e-mail address regularly floods me with the latest dirt on his most despised president. I know what is coming when I see that man's name in the "subject" line.

Conversation Dressing

The Internet e-mail networks have reminded us that every conversation has a "subject." Whether the words are written or spoken, they seek to communicate. And in communication swearing is a way we try to add weight or significance to our words.

Sometimes society asks us to judge with care our words. In a court of law we are reminded that our words need to convey the truth in order that justice might be done for those who are hurting and injured. For that reason we are asked to swear an oath of truth. No one likes to live with people who lie, but we all realize that is the world we have. Yet we need, at times, to be particularly careful to guard against the shadow of falsehood in order to find safety. So it is that we ask our public officials to be "sworn in," making sure that they will weigh their words well as they give direction in our communities.

Yet swearing carries several dark connotations as well. "Foul language," said someone, "is the effort of a feeble mind to express itself forcibly." "Profanity," said another, "is a way of escape for the person who runs out of ideas." When our sentences are punctuated with swearing it is likely that we have grown careless with the values of our lives. We don't trust ourselves, so we assume others won't either. Habitual swearing becomes an exaggerated way of projecting honesty we know is lacking.

Commonplace social swearing, especially when sacred or unholy images or names are constantly grabbed in, is also an indication that life itself has lost its sensitivity to God. When we lose our ability to pray but increase our vocabularity of profanity we are judging ourselves, not God.

Judging Ourselves

Several generations ago Robert Ingersoll built himself an international reputation as "the Great Agnostic" with his clever attacks on the Christian religion. For fees of up to $3,500 a night he would dazzle audiences with his caustic arguments. One of his favorite crowd-pleasers was a dramatic build-up that described the Bible's portrait of God as jealous of his honor and ready to strike down blasphemers.

Ingersoll would open his pocketwatch and in all the craft of showmanship, solemnly declare that he was about to curse the Name of Almighty God. In gentlemanly good taste, however, he would give God five minutes in which, as he said, "to strike me dead and damn my soul."

The excited and agitated crowds held their breaths in tingling amazement. Silence thundered as those five minutes dragged by, expanded to eternities in the dread of expectation. Witnesses reported that beads of perspiration forced themselves from hundreds of furrowed brows, and not a few individuals were supposed to have fainted outright at the pressures of the moment.

Then, in the calmness of his self-confident arrogance, Ingersoll would snap shut the watch and declare, "There! You see there is no God or he would have taken me at my word."

On a European tour Ingersoll performed the stunt one evening in London. The next day excited men from Rev. Joseph Parker's congregation tried to worry him with the news. But with a calm sense of faith Parker simply asked, "And did the American gentleman think he could exhaust the patience of God in five minutes?"

That was probably what James had in mind when he indicated that our penchant for swearing was a condemnation of our own small minds and hearts. Parents may get hurt when their children spit scathing names in a heated argument, but they know that eventually those youngsters will want to come home. The nasty words hurt the speakers more than they do the fathers and mothers. So too with with us. God may cry at our foul or brazen language, but in the long run we are the ones who grow smaller.

76

First Aid

"Is any one of you in trouble? He should pray." (James 5:13)

A friend of mine teaches ethics at a Christian college. Several years ago there was a scare on campus because a student had been raped. Since my friend wanted his students to deal with actual ethical situations, he began the next class session with a question: "If a friend came to your room in tears, telling how her date had just raped her, what is the first thing you would do to help her?"

After a moment's reflective silence one student raised her hand and asked, tentatively, "Pray?"

The whole class broke out in laughter, relieved to have a spot of comic relief to ease the tension. Even my friend found himself smiling and shaking his head slightly. "Of course," he said, "but *then* what would you do?" For the next hour he led the gathering in an ethical discussion of social care for someone who had been deeply hurt.

Second Thoughts

When my friend got home that evening he reflected on the class session and began to grow restless. Why, at a Christian college, he thought, should the suggestion of helping someone by beginning with prayer be greeted with laughter? And why should even he, an ordained minister of the gospel and a Christian ethics professor, initially wave off the suggestion of prayer as simply a polite formality to be dispensed with before the real business of helping began? Why should prayer seem so insignificant and powerless?

These are important questions, for in spite of our pious talk we often treat prayer with apologetic skepticism. When I was a seminary student, one of the elders at the church where I was working decided to make a career move. He invited the pastor and me to a demonstration of a product promotion speech he was developing as he began a sales and distribution job with a nationally-famous pyramid-like company. During our evening together he played a tape of a motivational speech he had heard at a recent company rally. The most gripping speaker was a former pastor who now was a top sales distributor for this famous firm.

"I used to be a pastor," the man said, "and all I had to give people was prayer. When I was a pastor I had a man come to me weeping for the tragedy of his life. 'I'm a poor fellow, Pastor,' the man cried, 'and it is ruining my marriage. I can't make enough to buy my wife the things she wants, and our children feel out of place at school with their shabby clothes. Sometimes I think I should divorce my wife, because then she would get more money from the government than she gets from me. What should I do Pastor?'

"I felt so bad," said the former pastor, now turned top salesman. "At that time all I could offer the man was prayer. If only I knew then what I know now. If he came to me today I could help him so much more!"

Beyond Coincidence

The crowd roared with approval, and applauded that former pastor as if he were God. I think of that man's motivational speech every time I sit at the bedside of a terminally ill cancer patient. I think of that speech when I wrestle in prayer with a couple nearing divorce. I think of his words when I pray with a friend of mine whose life has been mostly depression and drugs. Does prayer help? Is it more an exercise in placating my uneasy conscience than it is a true "first aid?" I wonder.

243

Yet when I look back over my years of praying and being prayed over I realize that there is also a larger picture to paint about prayer. For one thing, as Bishop William Temple said, "I don't know if prayer works, but I do know that when I stop praying, coincidences stop." So too I have found that truth in my life. Although I can't document every exact answer to prayer, I do know that unseen forces have often assisted me and those I've prayed with in ways beyond rational explanation. Even the medical community has recognized the healing power of prayer, as Dr. Lawrence Dossey has reported in several of his books.

Second, I think of the way that help comes best when we are children. I watched a young girl and boy collide while running through a hallway the other day, banging heads and falling backwards onto the floor. Each was stunned, momentarily, and then each looked around for a nearby parent. It wasn't until they spied caring mothers that each began a mighty and mournful wail. Not only that, but the crying from pain changed its tone when they each rested in the comfort of hugging arms—wails that earlier seemed edged with torment became whimperings seeking sympathy. A big part of prayer, it seems from scripture, has to do with finding our way into the care of a Father, even when the hurts and pains of life still trouble us.

A Test of Sanity

Third, I think that James is reminding us that we are not alone in the universe, and that times of trouble are times of returning to our truest human condition of spiritual need. James does not promise that all our fortunes will change because a magical prayer has been offered. Rather, he indicates that precisely when we are so troubled the natural place for us to turn is outside of ourselves and to God. As M. Scott Peck put it in his powerful book, *A World Waiting to Be Born* (Bantam, 1993), either we know the truth of our spiritual need or we spend our lives playing games with ourselves and others that steal the best of who we are away from us.

In Hendrik Ibsen's famous drama *Peer Gynt*, the hero of the story tries to find the meaning of his life by traveling and interviewing others. At one point he visits an asylum where "lunatics" are kept. Their craziness, thinks Peer Gynt, must arise from the condition that they are, as he puts it, "outside themselves."

Not so, says the director of the asylum.

> **Outside themselves? Oh no, you're wrong.**
>
> **It's here that men are most themselves—**
>
> **Themselves and nothing but themselves—**
>
> **Sailing with outspread sails of self.**
>
> **Each shuts himself in a cask of self,**
>
> **The cask stopped with a bung of self**
>
> **And seasoned in a well of self.**
>
> **None has a tear for others' woes**
>
> **Or cares what any other thinks.**
>
> **We are ourselves in thought and voice!**

That is the tendency within each of us—to become swallowed up with ourselves. Perhaps it is for that very reason that James says the first sign of true mental and spiritual health is this—if anyone is in trouble he should pray.

77

The Language of Faith

"Is anyone happy? Let him sing songs of praise." (James 5:13)

A couple traveling through Florida stopped at a beautiful mansion on the Gulf coast to take a tour recommended in their vacation guide. At the door they were given a brochure and invited to move through the grand old house at their own pace.

Most rooms had velvet ropes strung through them to keep people away from delicate fixtures and irreplaceable antiques. In the master bedroom on the upper floor, however, there were no barriers or shields guarding the curtains or plush bed coverings. Instead there were three small signs, one pinned to the drapes, one lying on the bed, and the third set atop an ornately carved chest-of-drawers. Each placard carried the same message: "Wash hands immediately after touching."

Contamination

Not wanting to be contaminated by some chemical in the room the husband and wife admired things quickly and from a distance. When they exited the house, though, they stopped long enough to ask the guard what kind of toxic preservative was used in that particular room.

"There's actually nothing on those things," he told them. "We just never had much luck with the 'DO NOT TOUCH!' signs."

Sometimes our Christian faith becomes a bit like that old mansion. We display our pious deeds and religious acts all neatly laid out, properly cleaned and pressed, set in place and shown to the best advantage. It can, in fact, take on a bit of a toxic scent. Ellen Glasgow, in her autobiography *The Woman Within* (Harcourt, Brace, 1954), tells of her father as a man full of rectitude and rigid with duty. "He was entirely unselfish," she writes, "and in his long life he never committed a pleasure." Too bad for him.

When former French President Charles deGaulle appointed a colleague as ambassador, the man asked for one last audience before traveling to his distant post. "Monsieur le President," he said passionately, "I am filled with joy at my appointment!"

Mr. DeGaulle raised an eyebrow, waited for a reproving moment, and then said icily, "You are a career diplomat, sir. Joy is an inappropriate emotion in your profession."

I know some Christians who seem to position their religion in a similar manner. They are willing to tolerate a bit of exuberance in new converts or teenagers who have had an experience of God's care. But for the rest they seem to raise an eyebrow and cast a circle of disdain that implies, "You are a career Christian. Joy is an inappropriate emotion in your profession."

Contentment

Not so, says James. With these few words he links the emotions of today with the expressions of joy found in the Psalms of the Old Testament. These were, after all, the language of faith that James' readers, Jewish Christians scattered around the Mediterranean world, would have memorized and sung in synagogue worship.

The word James uses to describe a person's delightful outlook is interesting. While the New International Version translates it "happy" and the King James Version gave it the rendition "merry," neither word conveys the full impact of James' choice of the Greek word "euthumia." "Well moved" might be a literal approximation, or "fully and enjoyably passionate" a decent paraphrase. It pulls together our ideas of pleasure, happiness and joy.

Pleasure is what we feel when something rubs our sense the right way. Pleasure is a good cup of coffee a the right time of day. Pleasure is the touch of a hand or the smell of steaks on the barbecue. Pleasure is watching the first big snowflakes fall or hearing the compliment of a friend. Pleasure has to do with our senses; it is our response to things that give us a buzz.

Happiness arises from our circumstances: a promotion, a raise, a first home, a new toy. While pleasure is our response to pleasant sensations, happiness is our delight at positive happenings. That's why the most popular song in the world is "Happy Birthday to You!"

Celebration

Joy rounds out the trilogy with the dimension of choice. While both pleasure and happiness tend to be our response to external things acting on us, joy is a decision we make as to our outlook on life. Joy has four aspects to it:

- Joy Starts in the Heart—it begins with the commitments of a relationship we choose.
- Joy Is Refined in the Mind—we choose to look at life as shaped by the strength of this relationship.
- Joy Expands with the Hands—it grows through sharing rather than self-gratification.
- Joy Come Out of the Mouth—there are more than 30 words in the Bible that can be translated "joy," with most of them indicating a manner of expression.

When a couple took their non-Christian friend to our worship services one Sunday morning, she stared in wide-eyed amazement at the strangeness of the things we were doing, right through prayers and praise and proclamation. At Sunday dinner they asked her what struck her most about the morning event. "The singing," she said. "You Christians do a lot of singing."

Exactly. That is why James says when we are deeply moved because of our relationship with God it has to erupt in music of the heart.

78

Practicing Medicine with a Better License

"Is anyone of you sick? He should call the elders of the church to pray over him and anoint him with oil in the name of the Lord. And the prayer offered in faith will make the sick person well; the Lord will raise him up." (James 5:14)

Fred was a big man with a big heart. His life had been ringed with tragedy, but he had grown through it and chose to spend his last career years as a missionary in Africa. A few years later he was returned to our town near death. A brain tumor had suddenly appeared and quickly robbed him of speech and motor control. He was hospitalized for several weeks and then released to die at home.

We prayed much for Fred. We shared the personal and family needs through a wide web of Christian contacts. We held specific healing services and added Fred's condition to our weekly prayer bulletin.

Gentling Death

In spite of our best desires we gradually became aware that only death would bring divine healing. Fred's life this side of eternity was too far destroyed for recovery.

I made regular visits to the small house that Fred's wife purchased. Mostly Fred lay in bed moaning and restless. While his muscles contorted horribly his skin began to turn unhuman shades of gray. Several times the family members, scattered at some distance, were called together for what appeared to be "the end."

On one of these occasions I stood with them in a circle around Fred's bed. Fred was greatly agitated, and moaned incomprehensibly. I read a Psalm and a promise from Paul, and then we prayed together, holding hands, asking God to take Fred home soon. It only seemed, however, that Fred's inner restlessness got worse. I stepped closer to the bed and placed my hand on his forehead. I spoke directly to him the blessing he himself had pronounced over God's people so many times: "The Lord bless you and keep you, Fred. The Lord make his face shine upon you. The Lord smile upon you and give you his peace" (Numbers 6:24-26).

Immediately Fred settled peacefully, his muscles relaxing and his labored breath easing. "You can go home now, Fred," I said. Each family member held Fred's hands briefly, speaking words of care release. I walked out of the house. Before I could drive away Fred slipped into eternity.

Anointing Sores

LaVern struggles with open sores on her legs, among several different ailments. She is in great pain most of the time, and alternates between weeks of sitting in a lounge chair with her legs elevated and periods of aggressive treatment in the hospital. We pray together regularly over the telephone, and now and then I sit with her for an hour sharing the whimseys of life. Few people I know have endured as much pain and heartbreak as has LaVern. Yet fewer still have developed as joyful an outlook on the many small graces of existence.

One day LaVern called me with a new request. She had been reading these verses in James' letter and wanted me to come over with an elder of the church to anoint her with oil. I called one of the elders and a trusted prayer partner, and we gathered around LaVern's chair. First we spent time confessing to one another, then we spent time in prayer. We shared the Bread and Cup of the sacrament, seeking intimacy with Jesus and one another in the Body. We touched the sores on LaVern's legs, and begged for healing. Then I took the oil and rubbed it gently over LaVern's wounds, commanding them, in the name of Jesus, to be healed. We gave God thanks for the healing he was bringing and would accomplish, and I spoke the same blessing I had pronounced over Fred.

Bringing Healing

There was no "electric shock" moving through my fingers or LaVern's legs, nor any immediate end to the weeping from the skin openings. Yet in the next week a remarkable change took place, both in the peace that infused LaVern's heart and the clear closures of the wounds. Her doctors put off scheduled surgery and several months later LaVern came to Sunday worship for the first time in a year, standing on her own legs.

LaVern's struggles with those sores have continued over the years, and she has called for prayer many times. Now and again we look back to the day we met together with the elders of the church and anointed her wounds as a watershed moment. LaVern believes she experienced a special healing in that moment. I think so too.

I also think Fred was healed in the moment of our touch at his bedside, though in a different way. There is power for life in the gospel of Jesus that sometimes works through the medical industries of our culture and sometimes works in spite of them. There is nothing in the Bible to call into question a Christian's use of doctors and prescription medications. But neither does the Bible tell us that doctors are the true Great Physician. Whenever healing happens, God has smiled.

79

Sick Souls

"If he has sinned, he will be forgiven. Therefore confess your sins to each other and pray for each other

so that you may be healed." (James 5:15-16)

I was working the sign-off show at a radio station during my seminary days. It was just after 11:30 one night when the telephone rang. A sleepy voice at the other end asked, "Is this that religious radio station?"

"Yes," I said.

"Well I'm dialing all over the place on my radio," she told me, "and I can't find your music…"

So I gave her the frequency of our signal, and then tried to engage her in a little more conversation. She sounded like she needed someone to talk with as much as she needed the music.

Betty's Blues

During the next twenty-five minutes her story spilled out. Much of it was an awkward tale of bad choices and bad times, more recently etched with both physical and relational pains. That night, in the dark and lonely places of her world, it all began to seem toom much for Betty, and she decided to end her life. She took a bunch of pills and now was trying to find the right kind of music on her radio. Then she would slip away exchanging my music for that of the angels. Or so she told me.

I tried to get Betty's address so that I could call the police. I tried to get her telephone number, but she would not let anything slip out.

At midnight I had to give a station ID along with headline news and the weather forecast before switching to a taped program. It would all take about three minutes. I told Betty to stay on the line, and that I would be back with her as quickly as I could. But when I picked up the receiver again there was no one at the other end.

I went home that night torn inside. Who was Betty? What had happened to her? Why was she all alone? Would she survive til morning?

Midnight Confessions

It was four nights later that my room-mates shook me awake at 1:30 a.m. There was a woman on the telephone. She had the number at our apartment but she didn't know why. When I picked up the receiver I knew immediately that it was Betty. Once again the world had gotten very small and dark for her, and down in her dungeon Betty needed God. Mostly Betty needed God with skin on. And that is why, when she found a scrap of paper with a strange telephone number written on it, she called our number trying to find God. And in the confessions of our second late-night phone chat Betty did find God.

Confession helps us find ourselves. Dostoevsky explored our need to confess in his powerful novel *Crime and Punishment*. We all tempt fate, as Rodya did in that story, pretending that we can get away with stuff we know is harmful to ourselves or others. Rodya keeps his public masks in place, all the while shrinking and shriveling on the inside. When he finally confesses to Sonia, she tells him he must take it a step further and confess to the whole world. His soul needs to connect with his tongue, and his life has to come back together through confession.

Seeing the Face of God

Confession helps us see God through the soiled tapestry of life. Walter Wangerin, Jr., remembers throwing a stone, as a boy, and breaking a terribly expensive light. That night at supper Walter couldn't look his father in the face and hated it when his dad called him by name. It sounded like blasphemy to his ears. Whimpering in bed that night, Walter turned away from his father's blessings.

The next day, when the story would no longer hide, Walter stood before his father expecting the spanking he knew he deserved. So he was totally unprepared for what happened next—his father knelt in front of him, hugged Walter like a precious treasure, and in his ear whispered over and over again the secret name only his father ever called him, "Ah-vee... Ah-vee... Ah-vee..."

In that moment, said Walter, "I saw the face of God."

80

Moving the Hands of God

"The prayer of a righteous man is powerful and effective. Elijah was a man just like us. He prayed earnestly that it would not rain, and it did not rain on the land for three and a half years. Again he prayed, and the heavens gave rain, and the earth produced its crops." (James 5:16-17)

When the nation of Israel came out of Egypt and met God at Mount Sinai there was a political transaction taking place. Israel had belonged to the Pharaoh of Egypt. Now she belonged to God. God had fought the Pharaoh for the right to own and care for Israel, and he had won. Just as prior to the Exodus the Pharaoh had specified the contours of his relationship with Israel, so now God did the same. At the top of Mount Sinai, God and Moses hammered out the political and social and religious covenant that would determine the character of Israel's future existence.

One element of that political landscape included the inescapable clause, "I am the Lord your God who brought you out of Egypt, out of the land of bondage." (Exodus 20:1) This was the declaration of sovereign authority. There would be no ruler in Israel except the God of the Covenant.

The Human Faces of God

Yet even this God would need mediaries. God would require human spokespersons to translate his glory into Hebrew speech. The greatest of all the spokespersons, of course, was Moses. Moses stood above the common Israeli crowd, a half-god hero, a leader without peers.

Moses stood at the helm of Israel's wandering ship for forty years, bringing her to the lights of Canaan's harbor. Then Moses died, and the navigational sextant was placed in Joshua's hands. Joshua helped Israel claim the new colonial territory on behalf of the Kingdom of Heaven. And when he died, the lines of authority passed into the care of the "Elders" of the people (Joshua 24). These older, wiser men were eyewitnesses of many of the great legends that created the nation of Israel.

When they died, the legends grew, but the faith wilted. Israel was adrift at sea, lost in a storm of international intrigue and factional dissension. A few powerful "Judges" managed to prevent the confederation from disintegrating all together, but it was obvious that stronger measures of leadership were necessary to bring the nation back to days of self-confidence, and a place of recognition among neighboring kingdoms.

Changing Times

The crisis of the book of Judges precipitated grassroots calls for a king. "Give us a king!" they told Samuel. "Give us a king!" they prayed to God, so long hidden. The outcome was the monarchy—established by Saul, consolidated by David, expanded by Solomon, ripped apart by Jereboam, and eventually whimpering into oblivion at the hands of the Assyrian empire (722 BC) and the Babylonian scourge (586 BC).

During the declining centuries of the monarchy, a strange bunch of men wrestled the spiritual leadership of the people from the hands of the political kings, often surrounded by their cultic priests. These "outside-the-system" renegades were known as the prophets. Some bartered their perspectives in the marketplaces. Some became wailing fixtures in the Temple precincts. Some were used by kings as *ex officio* advisors, and some were hunted down as traitors to the political cause.

Knowing the Mind of God

Yet the prophets became the *de facto* leaders of the people, urging spiritual chastity and calling for restoration of the religious and political and economic order established by the Covenant. Elijah was one of the greatest among these. He lived up to his name, which meant "My God is Yahweh."

Although Elijah was able to do many special and seemingly miraculous things, he is never portrayed as a wizard or some kind of superhuman figure. In fact, all of the miracles that happen when Elijah is around point only to God as the one who brings life and promotes healing. It is in this manner that James raises up Elijah as an example for us to follow when praying. Elijah wields no power; rather he understands what God is all about, what God's goals for his world are, and where to find the imprint of his creative and restoring fingers.

Elijah understood the Covenant stipulations that when God's people broke faith with God, he would withhold the needed rains until they finally came to their senses. Elijah was well-versed in the promises of God's Covenant that he would make the world blossom for the good of his people when they trusted him. His prayers were not secret codes the moved the tumblers of heaven's resources vaults. Rather his prayers were God's own speech become audible again in an age that had forgotten how to listen.

We often want prayer to be our magic potion that will force God to do our bidding. "Look to Elijah," James would caution us. "Pray like him!" No one can move the fingers of God until they have first absorbed his Covenant and his character and his vision, struggling like Elijah to understand the mind of God and living in a way that has put God's priorities first.

81

Come Home!

"My brothers, if one of you should wander from the truth and someone should bring him back, remember this: Whoever turns a sinner from the error of his way will save him from death and cover over a multitude of sins." (James 5:19-20)

James began his letter by addressing "the twelve tribes scattered among the nations" (1:1). It was a reference to the fact that the Palestinian homeland of God's ancient people, the Israelites, no longer beckoned. Instead, for those who are part of Jesus' new family of God, the Promised Land is found in Christian communities scattered throughout the nations of our world, and also in the heart-tug of age of the Kingdom yet to come.

Help!

George MacDonald helps us understand both of these homing calls in his children's tale known as "Papa's Story." The children beg their father, one cold winter's night, to weave again around them the spell of storytelling as they sit by the fire.

Papa agrees, and tells of a shepherd who brings his flock home late on a stormy night. One lamb is missing, however. So, after supper, the shepherd calls for Jumper the dog, and the two of them brace for the cold and wind and rain. Out in the hills they roam, calling for the wee lamb.

Young Nellie is snug in her bed at home, says Papa, but every moaning of the breeze echoes with her father's distant voice, and every whining of the woods is a challenge from the darkness that he must fight. She is frightened, for him and for Jumper, and for the little lamb they seek.

But this is a good story, a story of courage and rescue, Papa tells the children. Suddenly father is home, and Jumper too! They have found the little lamb, and have returned it to safety in the fold. The tests of the night have taken their toll on father. How weary he looks, and how torn and cut and dirty and bleeding is Jumper!

Hope!

When little Nellie returns to bed, her sleeping brings a dream. She dreams that *she* is Jumper, and that the little lamb is her lost brother Willie. You see, says Papa, a year earlier young Willie left home. He wanted to get away because he needed his own space, he told his parents. Willie couldn't stand the discipline of his father, and had to find his own fortune. Now Willie lives in Edinburgh and never writes. Nellie and her parents know, though, from the scuttlebutt of traders and friends, that Willie has become only a shadow of himself, cruel and greedy, filthy of body and mind, constantly drunk and lost in a mad world of sex.

In Nellie's dream she is Jumper, searching through the storms of Edinburgh's wilder haunts for the little lamb with Willie's face. The dream swirls around her like a mist, calling her into its phantom darkness.

When she wakes next morning Nellie knows what she must do. She acts on her dream and goes to Edinburgh to find her brother. Through hours of struggle and pain Nellie finally reaches him. He, of course, doesn't want to see her. Surrounded by his jeering and taunting pals, he laughs at his sister's foolish begging.

Nellie weeps at his harshness. Then she calls him by name: "Willie! Willie!" She tells him of his mother's broken heart. She gives him a letter of love, written in his father's hand. The scenes of home wash young Willie's mind, and the disease of wantonness sickens him. Before long, says Papa, Willie is led back home by his little sister.

The children enjoy Papa's nice story, as always. But there are two footnotes we need to know. First, the story Papa tells his children that night is actually the story of his own life. His name is Willie, and it was his own dear sister Nellie who, one day, years before, came looking for him in the shadowed dens of Edinburgh.

Second, George MacDonald gives the tale a subtitle. He calls it "A Scott's Christmas Story." And so it is, for the story of Jesus is not first of all a bland tale of pious peace or a study in theological ethics. Rather, it is a rescue story. According to James it is a rescue story always told best in the first person. Jesus came from home looking through the streets and alleys of earth's slums for *me*! For *you*!

Home!

And when we actually begin to breath the air of James' letter, it smells of home. Christopher Fry put it this way in one of his plays (*The Lady's Not for Burning*): Margaret and Nicholas are talking about a woman who seems to be acting strangely. Margaret says, "She must be lost."

Nicholas responds, wistfully, "Who isn't? The best thing we can do is to make whatever we're lost in look as much like home as we can."

That's what we do with our lives, isn't it? We have so many goals and dreams and hopes in life, yet so few of them turn out. We get old before we've done half of what we wanted. Somehow we never become what we thought we might. We make a few mistakes along the way. We disappoint some people, and they disappoint us. Even our best times have an edge of bitterness attached to them—when they end we walk away nursing our nostalgia. We're always a little bit away from home—from the home we remember, or the home we desire; from the dream we miss, or the dream we're still looking for. That's what Nicholas is saying to Margaret in Christopher Fry's play. We're all a bit lost in life. We're all a bit away from home. The best we can do is make what we have look as much as possible like what we think "home" should be, until we can finally see our true home, and, like James says, bring our friends along with us.

No matter where we go, no matter what we do, there must live in each of us a touch of that homesickness, or we die a horrible death. Our trips "home" are only a pale imitation of the place we belong, and merely a wayside rest stop on a restless journey to the real home of God's love, and God's eternity. More than we know, that is where we all truly want to go. And only in finding Jesus and the coming of God's Kingdom will our desires find fulfillment, and our longings be satisfied. Only then will our homesickness end.

Made in the USA
Monee, IL
04 January 2024

51077221R00144